Philosophy as Life Path

An Introduction to Philosophical Practices

Romano Màdera, Luigi Vero Tarca

IPOC
www.ipocpress.com

Philosophy as Life Path

IPOC di Pietro Condemi
3, Via Maddalena
I - 20122 Milan
Phone: +39-0236569954
Fax: +39-0236569954
ipoc@ipocpress.com

Original title: *La filosofia come stile di vita Introduzione alle pratiche filosofiche*
Editions: 2003
Publisher: Edizioni Paravia Bruno Mondadori, Milan

Printed in the United States and the United Kingdom on acid-free paper

ISBN: 978-88-95145-14-3

Front cover: Francesco Guardi, *Il bacino di San Marco con S. Giorgio e la Giudecca* (part), 1780. Gallerie dell'Accademia, Venice, Italy

Romano Màdera, Luigi Vero Tarca

To our friend Italo Valent,
a true philosopher through his whole life,
until the end.
And to our other friends
with whom we are learning
to do philosophy together.

Contents

Preface

The Actions of Philosophy: Self-Awareness, Political Love, and the Gaze beyond

The title of this volume announces philosophy as a style, a way of living, and elucidates its own endeavor: introducing, leading into modes of *praxis*, practices (in the plural) that can be recognized as philosophical. Two implications should be noted right away. In the first place, at stake seems to be no mere practical philosophy – a philosophy that, respecting the distinction between practical and theoretical thinking, would identify the problems of action and outline the rules to be applied thereto. Rather, prior to any subdivision securing the autonomy of "pure" speculation, as it were, philosophy is here presented as a matter *of life*, as a way in which life takes place. We should keep in mind this originary inscription of philosophy: far from aloof from life and occasionally applying itself to it, on a most basic level philosophy would belong in and to life, thus designating one of life's modes. Life can be inhabited by philosophy and give itself as philosophically inflected.

Secondly, then, at issue are those practices (those manners of action and enactment) displaying philosophical traits, those actions revealing philosophy at work: the actions of philosophy. What the "philosophical traits" of life may be, what philosophy "in deed" may mean, and how philosophy may "act" or "practice" are the questions addressed in this remarkable work. For the moment, let us anticipate, most minimalistically: the actions (or practices) of philosophy may be those that let transpire a spaciousness, a hesitation, a way of taking the time to hold life, right there and then, in attention. But let us briefly linger on the relation of practice and speculation, aliveness and philosophy.

1. *Praxis* and *theoria*, action and contemplation: most conspicuously in the last century, philosophical research of various descent has taken up the task of healing the rift between them and interrogating the apparent obviousness of this paradigmatic dualism. The developments in phenomenology as well as hermeneutics, in psychoanalysis as well as political theory, in ontological as well as epistemological discourses, in structuralist, post-structuralist as well as feminist debates, have severally indicated the phenomenal, practical, and embodied conditions of thinking. Through the emphasis on the experience of embodiment (indeed, on experience as such, as the undergoing, *pathos*, of limit) contemporary thought articulates a critique of rationality in its hegemonic, authoritarian, and even totalitarian aspirations.

The sweeping gesture of late modernity (or post-modernity, as has been said) has, thus, denounced and undertaken to dismantle the rhetoric of unified systems, the self-assertion of exclusive truths claiming universal validity, the strategies of objectivity and objectification at once giving rise to the self-mastering subject and the mastered object. While irreducible to a kind of programmatic orchestration, diverse critical analyses of conceptual privilege (and concomitant egotism) have variously invoked the need to free the human up for heretofore unheard-of possibilities.

However, as the Heideggerian diagnoses already intimated (despite Heidegger's own reluctance to take up the question of capital in conjunction with that of technology), one would do well to remain mindful of the resourcefulness with which the logic of the same can assert itself: it may operate with utmost stringency precisely under the guise of unconstrained freedom offering a kaleidoscope of captivating options. In this era dominated by the rhetoric of multiculturalism, by political idioms celebrating diversity, by the myth of velocity, production, reproduction, availability of infinitely many and equally licit opportunities – precisely in this era the risk of the tyranny of sameness seems to be most serious. Indeed, the rationality dominating the project of infinite objectification/production may be at work behind the quest for infinite plasticity, novelty, and originality: at once encouraging (indeed, creating) and preempting such a quest, making it empty and deluded. Reduced to the pure (that is, instrumental, mechanical) application of reason, thinking would, thus, simultaneously control and structure individual lives and experiences, exactly to the extent that it would comprehend them within its own all-encompassing logic. Reason would set itself up in sharp contrast to unreason (the irrational, the passions, affect in the broadest sense) only in order to subject it, in virtue of its own allegedly unaffected, non-affective hierarchical superiority. In this sense, what are called "emotions," "feelings," "personal experiences," would merely indicate what reason has ejected from itself, the specular opposite whose vacuity lies in its being structurally determined within the univocity of sense rationally imposed.

Under such circumstances, thought appears to be at once most constrained (anchored to conceptual platitude) and most violent: essentially disjoined from the occurrence of difference and multiplicity (much as it may *speak about* them), unable to undergo them and unfold in/as such an encounter. Thus, the world as we know it, in its mesmerized pursuit of the "new," of endless technological "advance," fascinated by means of communication ever more "multidimensional" and claiming to overcome time and space (operating in "real time"), may be the world in which thinking is not taking place or is most endangered, in which the word "experience" has become hollow, and the emergence of the ever-differing imperceptible. In the wake of such considerations, Agamben speaks of experience in terms not only of scarcity, as Benjamin did, but even of impossibility.

2. Thus, the apparent overcoming of the opposition between *praxis* and *theoria* may in fact reassert and exacerbate their being out of joint: far from being freed up for possibilities, the human being, at least in the North-West of the world, may risk the annihilation of *praxis* as such and the impoverishment of *theoria*,

reduced to the sovereign exercise of calculation. For Heidegger recomposing this dislocation and rescue experience in its possibility can by no means involve a re-articulation of the genuine problem of action, let alone a "rehabilitation" of practical philosophy. The ethico-political question remains for him inadequately posed because inevitably implicated in the framework of metaphysics, of philosophy itself in its failure to address issues more primordially. So profound is his suspicion vis-à-vis the compromising logic of the "first" (Greek) philosophical beginning, that the very language of ethics and politics almost never surfaces in his texts. For him, consequently, healing dualism means conceiving of thinking itself as action, *praxis* – not as a matter of application, but itself a deed.

I am underlining this venture of Heidegger's thought because of its vast and lasting influence. Even a thinker such as Derrida (clearly not to be reduced to the status of Heideggerian commentator, however brilliant and *sui generis*), who crucially thematizes the question of ethics, does so without drawing upon the resources of a vigorous, living sense of *praxis*. In this way his ethico-political reflection comes to be developed in its strictly aporetic dimension, in a constant effort to diagnose the necessity *and* impossibility of political practices. To be sure, the impossibility (i.e., conceptual groundlessness) of taking a stand regarding political matters by no means entails a paralysis: taking a stand (acting) will have been no less inevitable and urgent. Derrida's vital indication in this respect is that one lives and acts also *beyond and after* discourse, most notably the ground-laying discourse of reason. And yet, this insistence on the impossible as that which cannot be discursively/rationally exhausted continues to privilege discourse and hence to acknowledge possibility as a matter of discursivity. Otherwise, why would that which is rationally unaccountable have to be impossible? The living and acting that *also* exceed discourse can only exiguously (if at all) be hinted at, remain a phantasmatic allusion: beyond the concept, only dimly perceivable shades. Yet, what is at stake in pointing to living, to the living, in terms of spectrality?

In this line of thinking we find a genuine problematization of the virtually unproblematic practical/theoretical distinction, a problematization refusing simply to invert the order of hierarchical priority (i.e., privileging the practical) while retaining the two categories intact in their opposition. Still, life remains inarticulate, speechless. The unfolding of aliveness in and as action is surrounded by silence.

This is probably why, despite the fact that new idioms and concerns are now filtering into the institutional discourses of philosophy (idioms and concerns that would have been unthinkable until recently, signaling different sensibilities that cannot easily be reabsorbed into the "labor of the concept"), still, philosophy as an academic discipline, in its professional practice, abides mostly untouched by the doctrines it teaches. It administers itself as though its assignment, as is the case with any other discipline, were imparting erudition in classrooms and evaluating performances at the end of each term. As Luigi Vero Tarca points out in his introductory remarks, the distance is indeed abysmal between the teachings of the great philosophical figures of the past and the life lived within the institutions purporting to preserve and transmit such traditions. As though no longer able to reach out and *touch* life, or recognize its own being rooted in life, philosophical reflection seems to require conservation in a museum-like environment. As though no longer alive, philosophy seems to have become the inert history of itself – philology of culture, as Romano Màdera puts it, or, at most, the occasion for an increasingly refined exercise of demonstrative or refutative techniques.

The contrast between discourse ultimately discoursing about itself and life taking place in silence is noteworthy in its starkness. As noted above, the work by Màdera and Tarca does not present itself as a practical discourse, merely proposing paradigms for the structuring of *ethos*. It does not provide an account of life, which would (again) objectify life and miss it in its teeming proliferation. Rather, it seeks an acknowledgment of the intimacy of living and thinking that does not simply reabsorb *praxis* into thinking. Unusual in its aspiration, scope, and philosophical ambition, the research here presented *self-consciously arises from life*.

3. But what does this mean? Let us say that this work enacts a way of thinking capable of recognizing life as its element and, at once, committed to nourish this bond, to deepen the consciousness of its own exorbitant emergence. It points to the attempt to remain mindful of the experiential and corporeal conditions of thinking without reifying them, but rather cultivating the awareness of its own coming to be in their midst. This philosophical operation, then, explores its contact, continuity, and contiguity vis-à-vis the life of sensation, imagination, feeling – *vis-à-vis* life in its irreducibility to discourse, even in its unconsciousness. It explores its exchanges with these other modes of perception and signification. It *feels itself* as it surfaces out of the network of intersecting practices, involvements, and passions: transpiring from life, as its exhalation, its breath.

Needless to say, this way of thinking, of practicing philosophy, carries inherently political (and even politically subversive) implications, for it does not acquiesce to the alienation and desensitization prevalent in this epoch of global markets, "advanced" democracies, massive migratory movements, and the encompassing logic of production/consumption. It dares to reclaim experience in its possibility, indeed, as condition. It dares to re-acquaint itself with the figures and configurations of experience that, however inexplicable, nevertheless remain irreducible to silence, inarticulateness, let alone indifferent malleability. At stake is re-energizing the sense and felt experience of aliveness: feeling oneself live, as Aristotle said.

This way of thinking converses with life, not by imparting orders, but rather by listening and speaking in turn, out of affection. It trusts life, entrusts itself to it, lets it be – and gives back, offers the care and attention that may allow life to thrive, to reveal its own measure and realize itself in its magnificence. Of course, this is nothing less than the ambition, today nearly extinguished in academic circles, of the ancient philosophical schools (notably, but not only, Greek and Roman): the audacity to maintain not only that thinking and living belong together, but that their intimacy may light up in a dazzling splendor. Rather than assimilating the practical to thinking, viewing it as the work and potency of intellectual activity, the proposal of philosophy as a way of life emphasizes thinking as enveloped, however dynamically and irreducibly, in living. The invitation here is to understand their intimacy as a differential play, an ongoing togetherness-in-difference disclosing itself anew in each moment and calling for wakeful adherence. Among other things, this would constitute the sole ground and possibility for choice in the genuine sense of the word, beyond all calculus and egoic voluntarism.

Thus, prior to philosophy as either practical or theoretical, here we catch a glimpse of philosophy in its constitutive practical/physiological involvements, philosophy giving itself first of all as the conscious articulation of the living, in action. Philosophy as the pursuit of mindful living, or even ethics as first philosophy: nothing less is at stake in this work.

But still: how would such a way of life differ from, if not define itself in opposition to, the life encouraged within academic institutions? How would it announce an altogether renewed practice and understanding of philosophy? And what would be the implications of such an experimentation?

4. I first met the authors together in the spring of 2004, at what they call a "retreat of philosophical practices," near the lake of Garda. The retreat ran from Friday afternoon to Sunday mid-day. There were about 40-50 participants, mostly (though not exclusively) philosophy students at various stages from the universities of Venice and Milan, where Tarca and Màdera teach. Most of them knew each other already and had a long history of exchanges and group activities together, because Tarca and Màdera, both together and separately, for many years now have consistently met with their students, aside from and in addition to the institutional schedule of lecture courses and seminars. I found myself in a community of practices, brought together by the initiative of a couple of faculty members but evidently responding to a widespread and deep-seated hunger for this kind of togetherness: for the experience of being with others on the ground of the shared philosophical passion; for the experiment of feeling oneself grow precisely in virtue of sharing oneself with others; for the highly experimental venture of enacting the hospitality and comprehensiveness of dialogue. Indeed, the gathering seemed at each moment to find its form with

minimal or no logistical direction, "spontaneously" cohering around the collective activities and harmoniously receding to allow for individual spaces. As I had the chance to observe time and again, groups, just like living organisms, seem to find their measure in their own deepest recesses and furrowed fibers.

The retreat revolved around the theme of silence and included a couple of plenary lectures, sessions of meditative and corporeal work, activity in small groups or one-on-one, and time for solitary writing. The group reconvened periodically for experiential sharing and other contributions. Then as well as now, I could think of no other context analogously allowing for the integration of rigorous philosophical elaboration, biographical motifs, verbal as well as silent communication, self-reflection as well as extraverted focus, not to mention intuitive materials that, in their fragmentary and fleeting character, would on most occasions vanish unnoticed.

I will not dwell on the contents of the discussions that day: the silence of Socrates, who either listens or asks questions (the silence of his answer, which is not the lack of an answer, but the lived answer of his being there, of his quiet gesture); the spacious silence of non-identification with theses or perspectives; the intertwined questions of silence, emptiness, and predication, from Nagarjuna to the hypotheses of Plato's *Parmenides*; the reflections on the ecstatic mind by psychoanalyst Elvio Fachinelli.... Here I simply wish to underscore a few of the noteworthy features of this ongoing experiment in community. First of all, the group gave itself rules shaping exchanges and supporting their health. They involve:

a. the pervasiveness of biographical and experiential references;
b. the understanding of assertions as manifestations of the individual and his/her commitments/beliefs (communication not primarily understood as the alternation of competing, indeed, mutually exclusive positions);
c. exercise of hospitable listening (withholding the interpretation that does away with what is being said);
d. restitution and response by the listener, offering a potentially transformative perspective on what was said (anamorphosis) without replacing or ob-

scuring it (com-position);

e.   understanding the articulation of difference as never a matter of refutation in its destructiveness, and hence acknowledgment, containment, and inward examination of aggressive impulses. (Regarding this last point, note that, precisely to the extent it strives to obliterate, refutation is bound to betray, to miss difference in its radicalness and irreducibility.)

Ultimately, underlying the complex of these "rules" is the exercise of a heightened sensibility, a consciousness trained in the discernment of the various facets of each particular circumstance: the capacity to stay rooted in one's own experience and self-perception, while also open to another or others and to the innumerable environmental interferences, and hence attuned to respond and give back, in a spontaneity that is not unchecked, unmitigated (i.e., self-referential) self-expression, but the fruit of a continence, of a limitation dictated by the acknowledgment of the surroundings. What is at stake is a spontaneity constituted *ab origine* (at a cellular level, as it were) in the awareness that I am not alone, that I am who/what I am not despite those around me, accompanying me in this venture, but essentially *thanks to* them: the awareness that the other, alterity as such, is not limit, let alone obstacle, but condition of possibility – above all, not a limit of my freedom but the condition of my freedom and of freedom as such, in its vastness and comprehension.

The group gave itself rules, which are rules of freedom. For they are chosen and not imposed, the fruit of experience and constantly subject to experience: chosen in virtue of their being supportive at once of the group and of each – in virtue, that is, of their being *life-supporting*, encouraging expansion, magnifying the possibilities for each one and all to grow at their best. Again, it appears that the group finds its own rules in itself and recognizes itself in them: a "spontaneous organism."

We discern here the converging practices of awareness in the moment, of self-examination, and of communal sharing, in the all-encompassing perspective of the interrelatedness of all beings in the fabric of the cosmos. Quite crucially, indeed, this research draws upon the experiences of the ancient philosophical communities, approached in the wake of the exemplary work of Pierre Hadot (in a gesture that, far from nostalgic, retrieves what is alive in what is or appears to be dead in the historiographical repertory) as well the teachings of spiritual and religious traditions (more or less remote in time and space), in an effort to hint at the abiding question of the "mystery" that, as Màdera says, "comprehends and constitutes us" – as if to intimate that these lineages of inquiry and practice, however radically diverse, have taken their shape in response to *the same*, attempting to address and being claimed by that which is not exhausted and abides "unsaturated."

Perhaps the imperishable is not to be sought outside time. Perhaps eternity is not the prerogative of disembodied reason. Perhaps that which abides in its aliveness is not so much the a-temporal concept but the constancy of *pathos* (even as it gives itself in irreducibly plural shapes and bodies), the insistence of questions, the continuity of the experience of lives exposed, vulnerable, precarious, and yet belonging in the whole.

5. The present book arises from this experience, from this life, this living together, and offers it to everyone, anyone else. Discourse, most notably philosophical discourse, is always rooted, always starting from one (oneself, one circumstance), and yet also circulating, freely disseminating itself, wandering away, beyond any (self-)enclosure.

This work weaves together the motifs of self-awareness and communal cohesion, of friendship and political love, thus illuminating the essential intertwinement of biography and politics. Philosophy practices (enacts itself) as one (*this one, here*), and yet one is always constitutively plural, politically constituted. In this sense, echoing Hannah Arendt, we might think of the political/communal space as the stage on which the singular individuals paradigmatically appear: the theater of self-narration, where each is called to unfold his or her own *mythos*, to address the fundamental question "who are you?" Accordingly, we glimpse at the solidarity between the task of becoming oneself (achieving one's individuated, irreplaceable uniqueness) and political responsibility (responsiveness to the communal claim demanding that each one contribute his or her singular action).

There are indeed various intersections between the project here presented and Arendt's thinking – especially her insight into self-narration as *both* attainment of singularity *and* movement of one life beyond itself ("immortalization" of life in and as communal belonging), let alone her attempt to think the political by reference to imagination and aesthetic judgment (Kant). But what is unique to the proposal by Màdera and Tarca is their uncompromising attention to the unity of *zoe* and *bios* (life in its elemental dimension and life accompanied by reflection), to the question of their ever-nascent bond and, hence, of nature. (Parenthetically, it is when life in its naked materiality is not acknowledged as inseparable from ethico-political life that the turn to biopolitics becomes possible.) It is precisely in the attempt at integrating the dynamics of waking life and dreams, thinking and sensing, word and image, rational linearity and emotive impulsion, that the resources of psychoanalysis are variously deployed.

Thus, for altogether essential reasons, what is at stake here exceeds even the ambition to think the political space in its primordial structures. In the end what shines through this work is a vision of remarkable luminosity: the vision of the inseparability of life human and other-than-human; of the openness of the human to that which the human cannot refer back to itself; finally of a life so unfathomable as to overflow any humanistic construction. Beyond the *polis* and, above all, beyond the disenchantments with politics, a certain cosmopolitanism is envisaged: of a *kosmopolis* to be understood in light of *physis*, of all-embracing community, of the interdependence that gathers and orients all that is.

What transpires is, thus, a utopian vision – not, however, understood as the poietic imposition of a model (fabrication of the human according to an idea/ideal), but rather as the exploration of the possible, of a possibility at once human and not necessarily discursive, in brief: of *dynamis*, of the not-yet. Originating in utter situatedness, belonging in one *topos* (this one, here), this utopian vision may mark the difference between the affirmation of locality in all its conspicuousness and the captivity therein: it may signal the affirmation of place *in* the thrust beyond it. It may also be understood as what Fachinelli called the "gaze beyond": beyond "the conspicuous" and its confinement. "And beyond lies the terrain of mysticism. Not institutionalized religion, but mysticism as an irreducible zone, inassimilable and recalcitrant to religion itself. *Apex mentis.* Mysticism that is at the same time a *perceptive relationship*, which is possible for some, or perhaps even common to all."

Claudia Baracchi
New School for Social Research, New York

Introduction

1 An Experience of Philosophy, *by Luigi Vero Tarca*

"Concrete" is an abstract concept. We are often led to claim that we want facts, not words, but we ought to be careful of the *fact* that "fact" is a word. At the same time, words are also facts; indeed they are often among the most significant and important facts.

If every utterance is involved in this magic circle of the word, the same is particularly true of the idea that we propose here, which principally maintains that the significance of philosophical experience goes well beyond any objective, theoretical, linguistic content, as it depends in no small measure on the practical, existential context which is represented by the concrete life of those who do philosophy. For this reason, we believe that it is important to introduce, at least in part, an autobiographical element into this philosophical examination. This element, while remaining within the "abstract game" of words, nevertheless confers greater consistency and completeness on the whole discourse. It seems to me that the easiest way to go about this is briefly to point to the relation that obtains between the "philosophical theory" that I present in this book and a particular aspect of my real philosophical experience.

Since I began my career as a philosophy teacher I have been profoundly struck by the enormous distance that often exists between the teachings of great thinkers and the type of existence that those who are meant to pass down and renew those teachings lead, from within institutions whose mandate is to preserve and enrich that same patrimony of knowledge. I confess that for a long time I felt a great sense of trepidation (and, in fact, even now I sometimes experience a similar feeling) in seeing how school life in general, and academic life in particular, is governed entirely by hierarchical, political and administrative rules far distant from the principles of knowledge which, in my opinion, derive from reading philosophy, and which nevertheless constitute the official reason for the existence of such institutions.

I urge the reader to believe that I am very far from considering myself to be better than, or even different from, my colleagues; indeed, almost everyone I have met is enormously gifted both in the professional and human domains, and I am sincerely convinced that many of them are undoubtedly better than I, both from a cultural perspective and a personal one. And yet, all of us together, in our mutual relations, constitute a community characterized by a type of coexistence that is very far from any experience inspired by philosophy or wisdom. It is as if there were a deep divide between what we teach and what we practice.

My highly ambivalent relationship to that sort of life stems from this observation: on the one hand, one must consider that academia is after all the professional domain that I have chosen, and it moreover presents features that have a fatal attraction for me, precisely because of the presence of philosophy; on the other, the impossibility of consistently living a true, philosophical experience within such a domain makes this type of life in the end rather unsatisfying. Moreover, it has always been difficult for me to find elsewhere something that was truly able to replace philosophy. Obviously, many other important experiences have significantly helped, for example, those relating to Christianity, Buddhism, meditation, art, not to speak of the more personal ones that are connected to my affective relations with family or friends; nevertheless, these experiences always lead me back to a fundamental need for philosophy.

Almost automatically, this type of situation conditions an argumentative and "demanding" stance in those who are looking for some kind of consistency between "theory" and life, which leads to *demanding* that institutions conform to the values they are "officially" founded upon and that justify their existence. This claim, however, usually triggers a conflict between the promoters of such a stance and the institution itself. And, not only is this conflict almost always a lost cause for those who wage it, but it usually ends up pushing its promoters onto the side of wrong. Through their initiative they in fact worsen the nature of their coexistence, for rather than diminishing the pre-existing conflicts within the institution (which are in fact a symptom of its barely "philosophical" nature), they in fact introduce a further element of contrast.

I realized quite soon that any "struggle" bent on improving an institution would end up having the opposite effect. At the same time, it has always been clear to me that it was equally naive to resolve the problem little by little "from within" institutional logic, at least in as much as this logic remains defined by rules that are completely different from those that permit and favor the development of a truly philosophical coexistence. Thus the inconsistent nature of institutions seemed to block all paths that led to the realization of an authentically philosophical experience: opposition to an institution was contradictory and destined to fail, but identifying with institutional logic meant definitively renouncing those demands that were particular to philosophy, and forever distancing myself from what seemed to me to be the authentic goal of philosophy.

Thus little by little I began to see that the only way to satisfy philosophical exigencies was to find a path that was at once obviously different from the "official" path – which to me seemed wrong, or at least incomplete – but also different from any form of opposition with regard to institutional activity. It also had to include an experience that was in some way new and alternative, but at the same time able to maintain a positive connection with the environment from which it nevertheless in part had to distance itself.

It is worth pointing out here that this type of "practice" precisely exemplifies the philosophical point of view that I am expounding: to wit, if a thing that claims to have both a positive and universal value – and this seems to me to be at heart what philosophical knowledge aims at – is thought of as being different from the negative (in as much as it is positive) then (in as much as it claims to have a universal value) it must be thought of as different also from the particular form of the negative which is the negation of the negative, i.e. the negative of the negative. Only in this way will it manage to differentiate itself from the negative in a truly universal manner.

A whole series of initiatives was thus born, whose intention was to create forms of coexistence openly inspired by philosophy. Precisely because of their differential rather than oppositional nature, these initiatives have taken on variable, nuanced configurations and rhythms, and they have come to fruition both within the university – through particular work in seminars – and outside it, for example in the group of friends called *Liberi insieme* [Free Together], which attempts to combine personal, cultural and spiritual experience with social and political practice.

A decisive turning-point, however, came a few years ago, at the beginning of my collaboration with Romano Màdera, who had for some time already been a colleague of mine at the Università Ca' Foscari at Venice. One particularly determining event was when the seminar that I was holding at the university adopted rules that "its" group – now called *Compagnia di Ognuno* [Everyone's Company] – had already experienced most convincingly (rules that will be mentioned later on in Romano's introductory essay), as I myself had the opportunity to verify when I began to participate in the group. I immediately realized that those rules, which had amply proven themselves in guiding the group's meetings, substantively (i.e. beyond, for example, a few terminological differences) constituted a practical, workable expression of the same experience from which I had derived a formula at the theoretical, philosophical level.

Added to all this was Romano's great competence in the fields of psychology and psychoanalysis, not to mention those of religion and anthropology. His competence has contributed admirably to integrating my approach, which in the academic domain was largely tied to theoretical experience (I was a student of Emanuele Severino, whose teachings have formed a permanent reference point for me) and logic, which I also taught for many years.

Beyond this, I would like to point to two essential aspects of my relationship with Romano. The first is that our relationship has developed on equal footing unconditionally, and thus consciously and programmatically. What truly united us was the discovery that both of us were cultivating an incoercible desire to "progress by dreams" (the beautiful title of one of his essays), and that this, far from every abstract utopianism and every presumption of telling the world what it ought to do, meant to present itself as the concrete possibility of experiencing, here and now, a relationship openly and intentionally inspired by principles that we can easily define as "philosophical" (even if this term might sound reductive, for they could as reasonably be called religious, cultural, ethical, artistic, political or spiritual).

The second aspect is at least as important as the first. Our collaboration has always taken place within "group" experiences, defined by the principle that each person is the center of the group. What I wish to say is that our partnership, which might appear exclusive and peculiar from the preceding description, paradoxically derives its peculiarity precisely from the fact that our connection is all the stronger the less exclusive it is. Indeed, it grows stronger the more each of us sees how the other is capable of offering the same form of sharing, and thus the same deep affection, to every other living being.

Often, the tighter and stronger the experience of connections, and especially "group" connections, becomes, the more entrenched their opposition becomes to a common argumentative object, the external "enemy". Here however, the relationship between two people grows stronger the more it allows each of us to offer the same form of sharing and benevolence that obtains between us to all of the beings whom we happen to meet in the adventure of existence. For the principle that governs this experience is that every personal difference must be rigorously protected within the group's identity; the special tie that has developed between us (largely due to the fact that we are colleagues) is very far from constituting a preeminent or privileged value with respect to the other ties whose interweaving constitutes the life of the group.

What comes to my mind with regard to this paradoxical relationship – at once personal, concrete, and truly, universally open – is the dedication my brother Francesco wrote in Sri Aurobindo's book *Lo Yoga della Bhagavad Gita*, which he gave me as a gift. It reads: "To the brother among brothers." These words have always seemed wonderfully moving to me. With them my brother, my "real" brother, with whom I shared the intimate joys of childhood, but also all the pains of life's trials, literally put our relationship on the same level with those we have with every other living being. And yet this happened without me feeling in the slightest bit that the deep, peculiar meaning of our being brothers – i.e. the fact of having a unique relationship different from any other that we might have with whomever – was, I dare not say repudiated or disowned, but only even overshadowed or diminished.

I could linger on this particular type of relation and see in it the heart of my theoretical, philosophical endeavor, whose aim is to show that co-belonging (or, if one wishes, identity) between identity and difference, i.e. the positive difference between identity and difference, is essential for authentic philosophical thought. In the present case this means that the specific relation that two brothers have, and one that therefore is *different* from all others, manages to be truly "fraternal" in as much as the two recognize that it is *identical* to the relationships they have with every other person. Analogously, I could call Romano "the friend among friends," in the sense that he has represented for me the "prototype" of friendship that favors the birth of infinite new friendships of a similar type; for example my friendship with Igor, another "philosopher," helps me to I enrich my experience in a way that is as significant and intense as our ways of understanding philosophy are different.

The philosophical practice that emerges from this experience develops in an exciting, though hardly visible, way, one which is based on principles that are so peculiar as to seem paradoxical from the practical point of view: rather than taking the typical route of enlarging an organism, "conquering" external spaces, or acquiring new attachments, it discovers ever new affinities and "friendships." It is therefore a form of "world building" that tries to be fully consistent with the "philosophical" principles that inspired it. But here the consistency comes firstly from our willingness to recognize how far our actions usually are from total consistency, and secondly from our capacity to accept our "smallness" without adopting any punitive (and self-punitive) stance, or making us think that the undertaking has been a failure.

It is precisely this type of experiment that we have been conducting for a few years, particularly with the Open Seminar on Philosophical Practices at the Università di Venezia. Here too it would be interesting to discuss the matter at length and in detail, and it would above all be interesting if each of the participants could say what the experience of the seminar means to *him or her*, for obviously what results from my words is what it means *to me*, but for the moment I will limit myself to mentioning only one thing. What makes this experiment particularly significant to my mind is that, although it at first came about as the initiative of two professors, it has little by little become an activity in which our importance has been declining, not only because Romano in the meantime has moved to Milan, but also because its young participants have taken more and more seriously the idea of a company in which the identity of the whole truly remains defined by its ability to valorize the sensibilities of each person in the same way – which is much easier said than done.

As a result, the various participants have gradually taken more control over the times, forms and topics of our meetings. To take one example: this year, beginning from a series of reflections on peace, war and violence, a few women brought up the question of the types of mistreatment that we as "carnivores" – who nevertheless consider ourselves to be alien to violence – impassibly inflict upon animals, our poor "brothers" who live and suffer like us. Although this subject was originally far beyond our "philosophical" horizon, at least a fair number of us began to take it seriously as a fundamental question. In this regard, one circumstance that merits particular attention is that, though young, the women in the seminar have increasingly been taking on a greater role; I would even say an "orienting" or "guiding" role. And this has occurred *in practice*, without having been part of any project or "ideology."

And again, our meetings have been taking on the form of moments of real life which are often external to the institutional context, thus responding to the particular wishes and sensibilities that present themselves along the way. For example, we meet in the university gardens, whenever we can, or outside of class, in "typical" Venetian taverns, we take walks through the *calli* [the narrow streets of Venice], or we meet at demonstrations, or on trips, or simply in order to have a meal together, and so on. Even our very lively mailing list helps to make the relations among us continuous, and thus richer and more complete. In mentioning this, I would also like to underline the fact that, if I have given lesser importance to my friends in the seminar than to Romano, this is only because of the particular (theoretical and editorial) nature of the present situation, for their role (the role of *each* of them) is *truly* in every way equal to that of every other, including Romano, who however in the present context has a particularly important position.

It is precisely due to such traits that this philosophical practice already represents, for me, the realization of the philosophical endeavor that I propose here. Whoever knows me personally and knows what (little) I do with these friends, will surely ask himself: "Is that really it? That is all you had in mind by the above words?" Well, yes. "But," he might continue in disbelief, "won't this type of practice, if it truly aims to be philosophical, only truly be able to reach its goal when it acquires a public, official value? Otherwise how can one attribute a 'universal' value to such a limited experience, one that is so unfamiliar, so difficult to make one's own and that moreover in principle denies any enlargement?"

Well, I see a certain confirmation of its *rightness*, rather than a weakness, precisely in the limited, open and aleatory nature of our activity, which is due to the absolutely free, egalitarian nature of our groups. Any enlargement that denies the constitutive principles of our experience (as would happen for example if our groups assumed a *privileged* role with respect to other experiences) would constitute an enormous new difficulty, not a solution, with respect to the philosophical problem of constructing a freely shared world. If one holds that one's own experience can be generalized (for example through the adoption of rules or even of "theoretical formulas") and can therefore help others who are trying to do something of the sort (and there are numerous experiences, in many ways similar to ours, that I see sprouting up around the world), then it is clearly one's duty to communicate and make this experience public, as we are doing with this book. But this is far different from us adopting the criterion of "public success" as a measure of the value of our endeavor, and even more different from automatically interpreting any advantageous positions that we may acquire as a "success" from the philosophical point of view. Obviously, philosophical self-realization must bring "advantages," for example, determining what we might call a certain well-being, but the principle of "profit" that an authentically philosophical practice brings is that its advantages are automatically also advantages for *all* others; otherwise, however quickly one progresses, one always ends up moving away from one's goal rather than nearing it.

My philosophical experience experiments with the possibility of life being played as a "game" whose fundamental rule is full self-realization for all those who participate in it. And the contribution that I offer in the theoretical domain consists precisely in showing by what conditions such a thing is in principle possible. My hope is that this reading can help others overcome the pervasive superstition of today, which leads us to hold that it is in principle impossible for one's actions to conform to truth. Truly, one of the saddest aspects of the present situation is seeing how many people, who nevertheless harbor a sincere desire to achieve a peaceful and harmonious coexistence, are induced all the same to act egotistically and overbearingly out of the conviction that it is impossible to act in accordance with philosophical (i.e. "universally positive") knowledge, and that therefore adhering to philosophical principles is absurd and damaging to oneself and others.

My philosophical experience tells me that this conviction seems ineluctable only from within a negative standpoint, one which identifies the positive with the negation of the negative (for example justice with the punishment of the guilty, or peace with victory in war, and therefore with the defeat of one's enemies), and which deems a universally positive position impossible, precisely because, according to this hypothesis, good actions become by definition negative at least with respect to those whom one considers overbearing, violent, etc., and whom one therefore treats as enemies.

The philosophical perspective that I present here ought to show how this impossibility fails once one singles out the positive practice in an action that is different from a struggle against the negative, and precisely in the action which, in distinguishing itself in general from every oppositional stance, also distinguishes itself from the negative stance with respect to those who are prisoners of such a "negative" stance. The text that I present in this book – whose bibliography, for "autobiographical" reasons, consists predominantly of my writings (in which, moreover, one can find all the necessary references for further study) – aims to "demonstrate" that it is in fact truth (even the "stronger" truth, the one that is tied to necessity) which, far from showing us the absurdity of attempting to maintain an authentically philosophical attitude, "shows" us that constructing a better world *truly* is possible: it is *possible* to elude evil and the negative, violence and pain. And, in as much as it is possible, it *is* to be attempted [*è doveroso*].

2 Biographical Notes of a Practitioner, *by Romano Màdera*

Like everyone else, I encountered philosophy in high school, in the sense that it was only in high school that I began to understand fully what my father, my sister and my brothers meant when they said "philosophy," a term that was used at home as a reminder or a living reality of a course of study. It interested me, but, as often happens, it only grabbed me when incarnated by my philosophy professor at the Liceo Cairoli of Varese, Cesare Revelli. He was a genius of a teacher and a man who knew how to offer you the study of philosophy and history as if it was there that you would find the keys to finally clear up the mysteries of the world. The imprinting was precisely the exciting discovery that you could bring order, and therefore light and relief to the miserable chaos of an adolescent's brain and of a world that seemed unconscious of everything. And he gave us faith in the effort to understand. This recollection is not a nostalgic piece for a book of memories, or at least, it is not only that, for decades later, I am still persuaded that faith in the effort to understand and to explain is the most important resource at our disposal in any difficult moment of existence.

And yet it is precisely this love affair with philosophy that has led me, and many, many others of my generation, to question it: holding the nexus of philosophy-life of personal world-existence to be central to "philosophical discourse" meant furiously pushing ourselves towards the forms of thought that most dared to implicate themselves in practice, namely those of Marx and Freud. Later on, after 1974, when the last fires of political militancy began to die out for me, Nietzsche's work became central. I wrote my first book, *Identità e feticismo. Forma di valore e critica del soggetto, Marx e Nietzsche*, between 1975 and 1976, and it was published in 1977; the book, whose second part is entitled "History and Biography," is a sort of theoretical seismography of my trajectory. The first sketches of a biographical philosophy, "my" philosophy of course, were right there.

Biography, in my acceptation, was the theoretical figure that emerged from a critique of the subject (critically, I mean, with respect to all three thinkers, but with great debts towards them) rethought in light of these attempts to free oneself from philosophy as ideology, inaugurating a form of thought that was capable of reflecting on the things that condition it. This strange trinity could only be seen to have a common goal in the desperate critique of all of the theory's forms of self-referentiality. And this also meant that philosophy could not be reduced to philology and the history of philosophy, nor could it limit itself to some specialized critical analysis of language, however modest and scientific. Today I would say that what I was expressing backwards in that "anti-traditional" revolt was an unhappy love for the most traditional of the philosophical vocations, the love of wisdom.

Once I began teaching Philosophy of the Social Sciences, at the Università della Calabria, a certain hesitation and dissatisfaction with philosophy, taken within the limits only of philosophical discourse, continued to haunt me; indeed they became more acute. What good was the philosophy that I was studying, even when it was combined with sociology, psychoanalysis and a critique of political economy, what good was the type of philosophy that ruthlessly dealt with life, if they did not help to sift through the wounds of experience? Of course you could see the connection, but not the forms of mediation. The gap between experience and thought flattened the catastrophic particulars (insignificant for thought in their particularity? useful only as a sacrifice in constructing concepts?) that had to be lived every day. Whence my decision to go from self-analysis – which in my case had been rather inconclusive – to psycho-analysis, and Jungian analysis in particular.

In that domain, I had begun to read a bit about individuation, and I had found the fascinating expression "mythobiography" in the works of Ernst Bernhard, the founder of the Italian school of analytic psychology. This term was very promising for me, for although I knew nothing about it at the time, I had in fact called the second part of *Identità e feticismo* "History and Biogra-phy." Moreover, my analysis with Paolo Aite, in which we used "sandplay," has been the most vivifying intellectual experience of my life up to now. Whence my interest in following a path that combines experiential depth inves-tigation, with its methods of analyzing dreams and activating imaginal possi-bilities (the Jungian active imagination, but above all the construction of "land-scapes of the soul" in "sandplay," which was formerly called "world play"), and the holistic, universalizing passion of the philosophical vocation.

During my years at the Università della Calabria, in 1981 and 1982 espe-cially, but continuing until 1984, I performed a teaching experiment with senior theses, an experiment that I consider a truly renewed philosophical practice. I suggested to a few of the people who wanted to do a thesis with me that they postpone choosing their topic for one year, and instead commit themselves to coming every week, or at least every other week, to a personal interview in which they would talk about their biography, and if necessary, their dreams. At the end of the year we would have a topic for their thesis, and would therefore have translated a living nucleus of experience into a domain of theoretical re-search. This experiment was meant to broaden a guiding motif for biography, looking for its theoretical resonances, which could be symbolic as well as con-ceptual. The students would then proceed with their thesis according to the usual guidelines, and the final product would be formally indistinguishable from any other thesis.

The purpose of this work method was to find a strong motivation for the students and discover the vital force of theory, once it had been put back into direct contact with biographical excavation. I think I can say in all honesty that this attempt worked impeccably, at least in the sense that those who participated found both the method and the results that they achieved highly meaningful, and this despite its being nearly a form of wild psychoanalysis combined with an eccentric, eclectic form of philosophy. We had found a way of doing philosophy that was based on biography revisited as an increment of meaning.

Of the seven people who tried this method only one withdrew before the end, as the guiding motive that began to emerge was too painful to deal with. As Jung said – even if I did not know it then – in analysis, one learns almost exclusively from errors and failures; evidently this is true in philosophical practice as well. Even though it had no consequences, that person's withdrawal made me think about the risks of our undertaking, especially given my lack of preparation, and my fear in the face of the emotional storms that such a relationship could generate. I suspended these experiments upon my transferal to Venice, where the lack of a campus made this type of teaching experiment impracticable; that moment also coincided with the end of my own analysis, when I decided to undertake psychoanalytical training.

Those experiments were so intriguing however that they spurred me to look for a different access to *motivations for knowing* that would lead to a *biographical style* of knowledge, and a few years later, I undertook a new experiment with a group of friends. For years we told each other our life story, with as much detail as we desired and with whatever symbolic and conceptual amplifications seemed necessary. We were aware that the transmission and communication of what one thinks one knows always proceeds, in school and outside it, and especially in philosophy, according to an argumentative model. It is possible to disprove even a commentary on a work of art. Yet without conceiving our communicative rules differently, we found it difficult to talk about our own history and about the juncture with the knowledge that had accompanied it and that had marked our narrative structures. It was on that occasion that five rules emerged, like a container that made a certain type of solidary and non-competitive communication possible:

1. There must always be a connection to biographical experience, regardless of the type of discourse.
2. Statements by others must be taken as an expression of the speaker and of his or her beliefs. This means that communication distances itself from the opposition of arguments competing for one truth that excludes the other's truth.
3. In listening to the other, one must be open, which means that in listening one ought to suspend any substitutive interpretation of the sort that implies that what one has heard is only a cover for something else.
4. The listener's contribution and return must be expressed as an anamorphic offer, which implies the possibility that a different point of view uncovers other aspects of what has been said, and that these other aspects can be freely taken into consideration, or overlooked, by whoever is leading the meeting.
5. The temptation towards the destructiveness of argumentative opposition must be suppressed and silently and self-analytically re-examined.

Even experimenting with these rules worked. When our meetings came to an end (after everyone had presented his or her life story; only the last story did not have the full necessary space) I still had the desire to apply these *rules of biographico-solidary communication* to meetings that would maintain the biographical connection, but which would push themselves to transmit knowledge in the domains of the participants' competence and interest. This could have been the educational, didactic value of the rules. Beginning in 1995 another group of people, only partially made up of those who had given birth to the life stories, put itself to this test. Even now, meetings of this *Compagnia di Ognuno* take place according to the same rules, which have proven to work as a conduit for knowledge that is imbued with everyone's experiences, and has proven to be able to take in a diversity of knowledge types and points of view, and make them cooperate.

Meanwhile, in 1999 an agreement with Luigi Vero Tarca, my friend and colleague at the Università di Venezia, gave birth to a proposal to begin an Open Seminar on Philosophical Practices, which is still operating at Venice. What garners the participants' interest is not only the application of the aforementioned rules, but philosophical specificity, with its love of the search for wisdom. This collaboration with Vero has given my trajectory the decisive push for a return to philosophy as the practice of philosophy, i.e. as a path to life. More precisely, I should call this an attempt to renew philosophy. Significantly, the first text that the seminar commented upon at length was Pierre Hadot's, *Exercices spirituels et philosophie antique.*

In November of 2002, when we were specially-invited guests of the Libera Università dell'Autobiografia di Anghiari, we proposed the first Philosophical Practices Retreat, an experience that we repeat each year. The retreat's purpose is to unite philosophical discourse with philosophical exercises, understood as instruments for converting one's own life into philosophy, in order thus to reinforce the practice of philosophy as a path to life. With this basic difference with respect to the ancient schools: the project's unity does not derive from the dogma of a particular school, but from reference to rules of biographico-solidary communication that permit us to approach different philosophical schools or religious doctrines as a guide for the exercises and for a path to life, selecting them on the basis of the necessities, questions and prior knowledge of each life trajectory.

It is this formulation that I call *biographical ecumenism*, an ecumenism that in principle excludes no orthodoxy, but that welcomes any orthodoxy that recognizes the equal dignity of other doctrines in the life circumstances of other people. I think that this difference with respect to the ancient schools also concerns the different position of the individual within his or her cultural world (and here I mean the term "culture" in its strong sense, as all that life makes possible, expanding upon biologically inherited preconditions). Simply put: in pre-capitalist society, or in the period of capitalism's constitution, the individual realized himself by looking at his resemblance to an "exemplary model;" in developed capitalism, the individual, if he or she succeeds, at least in part, in escaping from the grip of the "mask of character" suggested and imposed by seriality and fashion, often tends toward the "individual harmonization" of his or her sundered parts and dimensions, seeking a form and meaning in his or her own biographical experience.

It goes without saying that these differences imply a different "philosophi-cal discourse"[1] that is capable of maintaining the universal in the biographical and vice-versa. But we must re-evaluate even the ancient philosophical exer-cises, and invent new ones. Open seminars and retreats exist to this end.

At this point it is legitimate to ask oneself what all of this has to do with philosophical counselling in the strict sense.[2] One might already have guessed that the conception of philosophical practices that we propose here is, in large part, rather different, and am I not interested in entering into the merit of the terminological debate surrounding this question. Nevertheless I must add that individual consultation is inherent to philosophical practices as a path to life, in the sense that consultation can be a part and dimension of them, as a precious aid to practitioners. Again referring to my own experience and education, I maintain a path to consultation that involves five modes of research, which ought thus to be present in the formation of analysts, philosophically trained, or at least those who adhere to the basic outline of this project. To whit: a) the philosophical tradition; b) the teachings of religious traditions on meditation and contemplation; c) depth psychologies; d) methods of autobiographical and biographical research; e) the rules of biographico-solidary communication.

In particular I consider firsthand knowledge of depth psychologies, under-stood as a biographical search for meaning, to be of great importance for the consultant: this seems to me to be a good way to avoid defensive intellectualiz-ing and the idealization of pathological states, which are among the most easily encountered risks. At the same time, depth psychology and the dyadic practice of biographical philosophy often meet beyond disciplinary divisions that often awaken the suspicion of having been built on the divisions of professional or-ders; they intertwine and overlap, especially if, as it seems to me, the depth psychology is thought of as an ethical practice, a "new ethics," rather than as the application of an inexact science.

---

[1] I here refer to Luigi Vero Tarca's essay.

[2] Subsequently, I have given the name "biographical analysis and philosophical orientation" [*analisi biografica e orientamento filosofico*] to my way of understanding synthesis through depth psychologies and philosophy as a path to life.

Philosophy as Exercise and as Conversion
by Romano Màdera

1 The Search for Meaning

Philosophy has always been a path to life, dictated by the love of wisdom. And yet, if we asked most philosophers today in what their particular path to life consists, we would discover that it tends to coincide with the path to life of professors: philosophy, as a path to life, has become the path to life of professors who deal with philosophy. If this is philosophical practice, it is no more than an exercise in study, in research, in teaching the results of one's studies. In most cases, the problem of the reducibility, or irreducibility, of the figure of the philosopher to that of a profession goes unnoticed. All the same, the love of wisdom cannot be a particular profession: it can touch everyone, independently of one's job, or the role one plays in society. Even the characters from books on the history of philosophy have been philosophy teachers only in certain eras, especially the modern one, and yet always with notable exceptions. This simple truth, proven by numerous legendary and biographical examples (from Thales to Socrates, Diogenes, Epicurus, Marcus Aurelius, Avicenna, Bruno, Spinoza, Kierkegaard, Marx, Wittgenstein), has been obscured for decades by the identification between philosophy and the teaching of philosophy. Though free, the philosophical vocation has in most cases been hampered for centuries by the forms that a nation's laws prescribe for teaching any other "scholastic subject."

Today teaching philosophy in schools is a rather thin occupational possibility, and this uncertainty about "professional openings" can become an occasion for re-presenting a crucial question for every age: What can the forms of philosophy be, in terms of practicing philosophy? A practice that is combined with a philosophical discourse, but not reducible to it?

Philosophy must certainly continue to concern itself with studying, teaching and writing in its capacity as the art of inexhaustibly questioning every piece of knowledge in every domain of knowledge. Loving wisdom means first of all feeling oneself spurred to go beyond every answer that is content with sufficient functionality. Wisdom sometimes requires what is useless, knowledge for the sake of knowledge, for beauty and the torment of its own undertaking. But wisdom is not without a world: the desire for it is born in the world's passions, behaviors, techniques, sciences and arts. Therefore the history of philosophy cannot refer to itself as the history of philosophy only, cut off from the earth from which it is born. At each moment it regains vigor from the world's questions, from the circumstances of the history of a particular community of people, from the daily life of individuals.

I believe that in our world, philosophy must be renewed, but in order to be renewed, it must depart from the limitations of a purely professorial practice and re-immerse itself in its larger vocation as a search for paths to wisdom. This claim will appear laughable to us, who are submerged by indigestible quantities of information and infinite opportunities for training. Even worse, the claim is anachronistic for important sectors of specialists who now think that the only valid type of philosophy is the one prescribed within the limits of the history of philosophy; it appears absurd for a wide, significant part of the philosophical community – we might say the Quineans – who assign to philosophy the task of being a science among the sciences, dedicated to generic problems across different scientific domains.[3] Philosophy therefore, as it is conceived and offered in this work, represents a different way of practicing

---

[3] A recent and notable example of this trend in thought is Hilary Kornblith's book.

philosophy, one that aims to renew it, by returning it to its original vocation, in order to blaze a trail of wisdom that takes in our age's questions about meaning.

To us, practicing philosophy means asking questions of meaning and the meaning of everything; it means feeling this question as an intense desire. Nothing less, and nothing further from the majority mentality in an age shaken by the loss of the myths of the modern which, for their part, had relegated religious myths to a museum of the spirit. But it is precisely this debt towards things that time seems to have abandoned, combined with the deluge of offers to patch up the frightening request for meaning, that requires a turning point. Even if the task seems desperate, we cannot escape it, for from the moment we ask for meaning, this very request seems destined to slip away: answers are infinite and reciprocally relativizable, and presumably also ineffectual.

We find ourselves in a frightening predicament, caught between the impossibility of silencing an insistent desire and expertly forecasting its frustration – a condition that concerns the individual as much as the group in contemporary society. The incredible speed at which technology changes in our civilization, where economic accumulation acts as center, motor, end and means of communication and search for knowledge, has made all other ethical and spiritual choices interchangeable, and finally irrelevant. Everything is permitted; only prohibition is prohibited; the only punishment is failure, is not being up to the performance, or choosing a performance that the market does not favor; the only sin is not reaching the (economic, political and military) scale of greatness that converts any atrocity into a necessity for the nation, the government, or global security. Even politics is subject to the laws of economic accumulation: any form of relative autonomy that a state exercises turns into an agent of global competition, and there are no institutions of global size capable of effectively influencing the destiny of a planet that is unified and subdivided by the economy, which might act as a corrective.

This process makes a form of collective, psychic scission inevitable, consigning every thinking, ethically-sensitive being to spiritual desperation. Never before has the history of humanity universally proclaimed the rights of each individual to a dignified, free, material and moral life. Every type of racial, ethnic, sexual, generational, social, religious and political discrimination was condemned in 1948 by the United Nations' Universal Declaration of Human Rights, which was enlarged and deepened by other, more specific declarations in the second half of the 20th century.

There is a common mentality developing that is so strong it forces even those responsible for serial crimes against humanity to try to depict themselves as victims of some other violence. Whoever violates the charter on human rights implicitly and explicitly refers to that same charter in order to justify himself. An astounding leap forward in the collective moral consciousness of the species has thus occurred, a marvelous wingstroke that leads away from the abyss into which the horrors of colonialism, racism, social exclusion, global and regional wars, genocide, Nazism and fascism, imperialism, and Stalinist Communism had plunged humanity in the last two centuries. Precisely for this reason waking up from the dream of free, balanced, solidary coexistence is every day more bitter and desolate, a dream continually fed by the principles of universally recognized right.

Think, judge and wish for the opposite of what you ought to, and what you must want to perform every day: live in opposition to your ideals, contribute to injustice, starve the poor, deport the foreigner, deride the just, bend before the strong, take advantage of the weak, compete against your brothers and sisters, adore all possible idols, erase necessary anxiety and pain, serve up the lie of the day and wear yourself out trying to cure the incurable, as long as you do not have to see it. These are the counter-commandments of the law that accumulation imposes in a totalitarianism that is masked by official "longing-law," and whose law is to follow desire, whatever it may be.

This is the fundamental task of philosophical *renovatio*: escaping the death sentence that hegemonic culture secretly assigns to every search for meaning, condemning it to the vanity of make-up on the disfigured face of humanity.

2 The Biographical Method as a Universal Path

Freedom for all is freedom for everyone, and "everyone" is the most universal term, for it includes every other specification of power, possession, people, gender, generation. The Universal Declaration of Human Rights centers on the repetition of the formula "everyone," because everyone holds universal rights. This principle is often criticized, for one can argue that it descends from the universality that is specific to the modern, liberal individual, who denies those ways of life that are only possible in communities, thus side-stepping and negating them. One can in fact conceive of the individual as a bearer of a biography in abstract isolation from the historical and relational conditions that make him or her exist and become that which he or she becomes. Here, however, we propose a conception of the individual that gathers into a very special unity the richness of his or her social, and broadly cultural, determination. Again, it is precisely our respect for this special, individual quality which makes us look suspiciously upon a return to a notion of truth that smacks of forced approval, upon anything that holds for everyone, and therefore for no one.

Now, this suspicion can be overcome if one really conceives of truth as a truth that gathers everyone's truth. We might ask, "What happens when these truths are contrasting, when a conflict erupts? When conflict already lies within the individual, as is typical of modern individuality?" The truth that we invoke here does not of course consist in suppression, repression, negation, or even more radically, in denying the existence of the conflict itself.

The first difficult hurdle is acceptance. Looking more deeply at a conflict, or better, looking at it from the biographical perspective of unrepeatable individuality, can lead to the discovery that we mistakenly, thoughtlessly overlap observational perspectives. If, on the other hand, we carefully consider the perspective, and see its content as what constitutes the perspective and what it has implied, then the conflict no longer appears as an attempt to negate a certain content in order to establish another in its place, but as an act of force that tries to obscure altogether the possibility of differing points of view and contents. Indeed, we might say that the suffering that results from this acceptance consists precisely in this: according to its own criteria, each part, each dimension, each point of view has in itself its own truth and its own justification, if we bother to look at it deeply. Since Faust, it is here that one's several souls seem to shred the indivisibility that lives embryonically in each individual history.

Philosophy, even if it is veiled by a certain haughtiness, too quickly leaves these torments to the experience of individual lives, and loses interest in them, for it is unable to proceed scientifically. Unless it subsequently returns to them with tablets of laws that are inadmissible to the divided, conflictual modern spirit, tablets written in a language that is foreign to this humanity's psyche. They in fact continue to model themselves for a pre-modern reception that was adequate for individuals formed according to an exemplary model, and who found (or failed to find) their fulfillment precisely in this authorization.

But taking action based on the diverging impulses that contend for the same life is only the very first step. It records torment, but does not yet reflect it, and even less search for a possible alternative composition.

Biography is not simply something that is lived, nor is it a collection of lived moments. And moreover, something that is lived is often an interior, confused, undecipherable movement, an undefined emotion. From this tension we can begin to perceive a common tonality, a sentiment, or various distinct emotions that have not yet been articulated into images, nor into a collection of images that represent them. A word, a name or a discourse does not necessarily correspond to an emotion, a sentiment or even to an image. This does not mean that it is impossible to see a meaning in a sequence of images, i.e. in a representation without words. Images that, by their realization, are linked to emotional – and therefore somatic – events, images that do not represent external reality, but possible mediations between available facts and actions that could be imagined, carry with them the richness of all experience, and of all experiences. This is a process that is difficult to access if the experience is preformed in an exemplary circuit of exercises and techniques that is given to all. Moreover, this process was a most venerable cultural model, highly valued for centuries, which it would be remiss to ignore or undervalue: religious traditions, and even ancient Greco-Roman philosophy, have been woven onto such a weft.

Even today this type of path to wisdom has an important following, at least in as much as it has influenced Christian theologies and practices, and has been absorbed by Judaism and Islam as well.

We may explain the fact that this survival is tied to certain religions by noting that these religions have in various ways maintained an approach and a discipline that are concerned with the body and with emotions, thus lending themselves more to individualization than the bodiless universality of the conceptual verbality of modern and contemporary philosophy. Philosophy's strong individual character (each thinker has his own philosophy) is consigned instead to pure discourse.

It is a common sociological observation that in the last few decades the spreading of beliefs and spiritual practices of differing origins has been marked by an individualizing turn, with a more or less syncretic spectrum of support.

An explicit tendency in the so-called "new religions" and in the vagary of the new and next age, shows its energy by assimilating itself to the most rigid traditions. With a certain conviction, or with resignation marked by the anxiety of losing one's following, all religions and faiths allow each person to adapt for him or herself doctrines that have been established for centuries, often in difficult mixtures of beliefs. It would be pointless to look at these processes with moralistic superficiality, lumping everything together as the religious froth of a society of spectacle. Not that this motivation is absent, quite the contrary. But it is not enough. It is of capital importance to recognize the general tendency subtending the whole of modernity, or, more precisely, the entire civilization of economic accumulation: the rupture of direct, communitary ties (the neighborhood, the extended family, political relations organized according to personal ties) has been replaced by the exuberant growth of social ties that are mediated by the anonymous exchange of things and functions, and therefore by the dominion of money that must increase in order to reproduce itself and the populations that depend upon it.

Thus a new type of social structure has arisen, based on functional relations, and mediated by things or proceduralized connections, as in the division of labor. The family remains the only domain of direct relations in which a certain function and cooperation are still immediately tied to certain individuals, at least in the consumption of income. And the family has shrunken to include only the couple and their children; all other parental ties have loosened. In the last fifty years this has even been reconstituted as temporary monogamy, or mono-andry, which turns into polygamy or polyandry over the course of one's life.

However one wishes to judge this development, it is obvious that it represents a further restriction and weakening of direct personal ties within the whole social network. Thus a highly individualized society has come into being *because* it is built on impersonal ties. We find ourselves with a divided soul that makes itself heard first in the proud conquest of freedoms that the preceding history had not raised to the status of rights, and second, for the other and opposed dimension of this same evolution, in an oppressive feeling of being reduced to interchangeable atoms, to a terminal sensor for the development of infinitely distant and complex processes. All of this has had a paradoxical and critical effect: the birth of individuality, which only modern capitalism has made possible, heightens each person's sensibility to freedom precisely at the moment when it strips it of the transparency of the dimensions of one's daily life, which in turn are maintained by complex, anonymizing movements. The same thing happens to interiority: its movements become opaque to the subject that experiences them; they become exponentially more entangled, in step with the growth of possible, external influences, but also with respect to alternative ways of reading lived experience.

If the society of individualization proposes biography as a possibility for constructing meaning (and this possibility seems to be the only one that is fully adequate to the spirit and interests of our time), it also makes it a highly complex task. Possibilities for biographical construction in fact arise where the history of life is no longer predestined to flow in the riverbed of a few, well-defined exemplary models. The consistency and success of a biographical account therefore appear as potentialities which are constantly submitted to destructive entreaties. But, inversely, it is precisely the divergence of stimuli and chronically activated urges which, without being subject to any unitary conditions of meaning, dictate that any more or less reflected history of individual life arise in order to survive social requests and the need to make intra-psychic conflicts compatible among themselves.

The modern "everyman," structured in a dynamic domain, put into tension and form by the potential to form the history of his own individual life, and by the need to build it in order to compose disparate, divergent impulses, finds himself with a biographical task, and forced to respond. He is allowed to choose, thus dedicating himself to the uncertain task of testing himself in a self-portrait that recounts his journey, whose destination is the very emergence of his trace, profile and face from the immense backdrop that closes and nullifies each single life within its depth. The emergence of a sign that says, "I am the person who has seen these worlds in such and such a manner, and has belonged to them in such and such a manner." Or he may think he has succeeded in escaping, he may refuse the challenge, or lose himself in the serial segments that are produced to adapt to every eventuality of life, risking only mass games.

Even the philosopher must choose; indeed it is above all the philosopher who chooses consciously and responds with a work (the work of life) that far exceeds its written or didactic component: the risky work of biographical construction, or its motivated renunciation and assimilation to the collective backdrop.

The communion of truth and freedom that historical preconditions offer us in the shape of an open, and forever threatened possibility is therefore translated in biographical work, which the love of wisdom – forever the philosopher's vocation – assumes and solicits. A renewed philosophy can dedicate itself to the service of biographical work.

3 Philosophy and Care for the Soul: Comparing Different Faiths

From its origins, philosophy has cared for the soul; innumerable ancient texts testify to this. The soul often appeared as the microcosm of the macrocosm. One of the monuments of this conception is Plato's *Republic*. Knowing the soul meant knowing the world, which the soul re-presented by representing and acting the world in itself. The dimensions of nature, power, divinity and the soul appeared indivisible. Indivisibility is different from indistinguishability. Originary care for the soul is the non-negotiable dimension through which a given philosophy may even today attempt to fulfill its vocation.

As we have said, however, the conditions have changed greatly. The infinite possible worlds that have opened up to our gaze make it improbable, or only apparently practicable, that we will be able to re-use exemplary models to give form to the characters of souls in search of justice and the good. The social dynamics that produce continual divisions demand the opposite path as compensation: a complex individual harmonization. Can we perhaps dare such a reversal? Is it perhaps in the mirror of biographies, however delicately they may recompose themselves, that the worlds, in their image, may return to recognizing the harmony, which in spite of the forces of disintegration, holds them back from the chain of divisions that would dissolve their every form? We move from the truth of the unity of the world, the foundation of spiritual exercises for souls intent on self-edification, to the truth of the uncertain work of biographical construction for souls intent on the even more uncertain quest to reconcile worlds.

However much it may continue to shine through the backward world of modernity, the light of the original philosophical vocation has been transmitted to us deeply marked by its many encounters. Moreover, we cannot deny their existence without giving ourselves over to the illusion of being able to jump beyond a past that has come down to us in our soul's very nerve endings. We thus encounter the variously articulated web of philosophical-religious symbiosis that has been historically determined in the osmosis between the Greco-Roman and Judeo-Christian-Islamic religious traditions. Theoretical speculation joins with theological speculation, almost transforming itself into an auxiliary instrument. One may perhaps follow in the tracks of ancient care for the soul by accepting that they were calqued on ascetic, mystic disciplines: first on monachism, then on the spiritual exercises of every lay and clerical *itinerarium mentis in deum*. In the period from the 13th to the 17th centuries, which witnessed the transformation of civilization into one of economic accumulation, the re-emergence of an autonomous philosophical activity contained in its genetic code the languages, categories and problems inherited from the late-classical and medieval theological spirit. It is clearly still in this light that both the impassioned debate against Christianity, dating from the end of the 18th and 19th centuries, and the whole, still current, critique of metaphysics must be understood. I would even say that the rediscovery of metaphysics considers its undertaking to be credible precisely because the philosophical metaphysician has gained greater autonomy from the theological metaphysician. Nevertheless, a great part of the care for the soul, as it was understood and practiced in the ancient and original philosophical vocation (which, moreover, even then descended from a preceding union with religiosity and with its essential ritual and mythic nature), has remained, throughout these peregrinations, almost exclusively the task of religious teaching.

If for the stoic, physics itself was marked by its finalization towards spiritual exercise, today the philosopher investigates his or her own knowledge at the epistemological edge of the sciences and offers it to the logical instrument they imply. Something similar occurs in the human and social sciences. Attempts to confront the age's content-based arc of vital tensions arise for politics and public ethics, consistent (but in a few cases self-consciously so) with the destiny that has tied philosophy to the lay schools of nation-states. Even once a method of caring for the soul through speech – the *talking cure*, as psychoanalysis's founder called it – was born – not coincidentally of medicine and psychiatry – philosophy's position with regard to it was to take its scientific qualifications into particular consideration.

In short, philosophers seem to be limiting themselves ever more to the domain that stretches beyond forms of knowledge that have their own, collectively recognized relevance, towards a group of defined contents and methods, as if pursued by a sense of remorse for an ancient claim of supremacy, and by a sense of inferiority with respect to science's autonomous successes. They seem as if they were running behind a convoy that they are unable to reach, or on which they end up becoming a sort of curious anomaly. Worried by the accusation of being jacks-of-all-trades, philosophers internalize the age's commandment and become the most obsessive guardians of specialization and of the disciplinary legitimacy of any type of research. Philosophy's task has never been to produce all forms of knowledge: its undertaking has forever been to unify forms of knowledge. Many philosophical expositions can be read as discussions about what could be the richest, most appropriate, and at the same time most comprehensible and productive form that is able to give unity to different domains of culture, while still posing new questions.

What has dramatically changed, been turned upside-down in fact, is our relation to the branches of the cultural configuration within which we live and think. As long as configurations that tended toward traditional equilibrium dominated – configurations that were therefore suspicious of every innovation in the social and technical division of labor – the function of the unification of the world and of the soul needed no legitimacy. There was rather a certain competition within a given religion, among various religions, or among various religions and philosophies, depending upon how much divergent thought was tolerated. The opposite is true today. If the philosophical task wishes to remain faithful to its original vocation of being the specialization that seeks the unitary figure and harmonization of totality, of the parts of single units and within those units, it must begin by being aware that it goes against the grain of the times.

And here we already have a paradox: whoever wishes to unify, by his or her very presence, ends up dividing, and opposing a collective tendency. What comes to my mind in this regard is the Taoist fairy tale of the sorcerer who was called in to cure the ills that were devastating a village. Rather than getting down to work by visiting the ill, the sorcerer isolated himself in the surrounding area, protecting himself from the contagion and at the same time keeping up with his task. Eventually, the village was cured, at which point the sorcerer entered it. Clearly, isolating oneself does not go at all against the grain; on the contrary, up to a certain point, it is the very spirit of specialization and of innovation in specialization. It is thus a sort of homeopathic medicine: philosophy may return to cure the soul and the world if it investigates its principle task without letting itself be distracted.

As I said, undertaking a cure cannot, nor does it wish to, jump beyond its own history: it would lose many of its possibilities and much of its richness if it did so. I repeat: this philosophical practice persists in a renewal that concerns the whole tradition, and it seeks a unifying matrix that would once again present it as a recognizable, coherent figure, answering to the deep needs of the times. Philosophy's task is therefore different from classical service to a faith or a theology; not by definition, but because the situation requires it. Whatever the religion may in fact be (or that form of religiousness inherent in refusing all religions), it has lost, or is losing, the legitimacy that came with being transmitted from generation to generation in a homogeneous environment, whether the family or community, or more largely, the nation-state.

Whether we like it or not, we necessarily compare all beliefs in a world where every regional belonging is a dynamic, functioning part of a global whole. This does not mean, however, that we should dilute every belief in an indefinite, insipid broth. The discernment of one's own time urges each faith to look for the affirmation of its truth by considering the truth of other faiths. In this delicate task of integrating, reconsidering, reformulating the ancient paths to meaning, a philosophy centered on *biographical ecumenism* (etymologically: the communality of all those who inhabit the planet together) acts as a possible dialogue, link and communication. It proposes a criterion for confirmation and choice which makes use of living experience and, in the plurality of paths, alludes to a silent, mystic concordance with all those who and all that which allows itself to be joined to the widest and deepest tolerance, to respect for others' dignity and right to expression.

In proposing to recognize universally the beginning and end of agreement (whose task is to care for differences), this form of philosophy celebrates both its dedication to the most welcoming image of wisdom and its friendship and consent for what religious experiences and speculation by all faiths have always pointed to as the ultimate, ineffable mystery, the unspeakable essence of the divine, the highest symbolic place, where all names must be silent and all images must go beyond themselves. This is also the site of perfect equality among all differences, of the absolute communion of all types of speculation, faiths, beliefs. Deepening every path leads to a recognition of mystical agreement that marks the possible dimension of perfect confluence for individual biographies and, as such, also acts as an ideal of reason, the asymptotic point of infinite nearing.

Once again, the mystic unity that can be reached by elevating and plunging the soul into itself and the other (the forms of desire that move experience, and their reflection up to the point of fulfilling or cancelling every desire) demonstrates the most concrete realism, and orients the continual fission of society and psyche. All the same, it not only represents its countertrend, or ideal compensation, but also brings forth its own tension, i.e. the tension of unification that secretly governs the furthest, and opposed folds of dominant *glocalism*.

The soul and the world cannot be sundered; their co-belonging forbids it. Even the ancient dualistic doctrines – but the "scorn for the world" often brings even monists close to these doctrines – can be taken as transforming determinate conditions of existence. It is in this effort of the soul and the world (in the space and time of geography and history, of biology and behavior) that philosophy can find its vocation, one that distinguishes, but does not separate, it from both religion and psychology.

4 Philosophy and Care for the Psyche: Interaction with Depth Psychologies

By carefully considering biography, philosophy can once again find its vocation of caring for the soul. In saying this, I do not intend to replace any psychological therapies. Perhaps I should speak of complex interaction instead. Up till now, philosophy has dealt purely epistemologically with categories of knowledge that were more or less scientific, hermeneutic, analogical and symbolic, and which included psychoanalysis, psychotherapy and psychiatry. We have seen that the cost of this drastic limitation is the loss of contact with immediate lived reality and with the reflexive questions that arise from it. In an age characterized by individualization, distancing or repressing one's own passions in their effectual circumstantiality amounts to making one's own words impossible to listen to.

I do not of course mean that we ought to consent to trends of the time; rather, what is at stake is our ability to listen to and understand them, even if our aim is to overcome them. Such that we might suspect an unconscious collusion that claims to free true knowledge from every type of vital implication; thus life, blinded by every one of its own lights of knowledge, loses every chance of directing itself away from the "present state of affairs." Philosophy thereby dissipates, it lifelessly draws a pattern that it is no longer able to judge, once it has forgotten its roots and neglected to follow its perennial, fundamental task. Even for this timid yet proud effort by philosophy to pull back, every dramatic, singularly lived search for meaning has had to dig its own space in traditional religious doctrines, or it has had to turn itself into a pathology, in order to legitimate its care for itself.

One of the most typical hallmarks of our world is the desire to confront the work and suffering of life, not only to taking care of them, but forcing ourselves to cure them. All the same, we are not required to submit ourselves to this trend without trying to come up with alternative solutions. If, according to Freud, neurosis and psychosis are conditions that prevent us from loving or working, then we may say that asking that we carefully consider and reflect on the difficulty of leading our own existence (the *normal* request of every thinking being at a time of individualization and impersonally functional social ties) improperly meets the psychotherapeutic request.

There is no need to build new disciplinary divisions; our subject should rather encourage depth psychologists to clarify and differentiate their objectives and techniques in relation to different types of therapy. It is certainly not a coincidence that, from Jung to Bion, to name only two great examples, a certain unscrupulous self-reflection on what often happens in therapy has led to referring to "meaning" as the deepest therapy, and of psychoanalysis as a type of new, re-established "anthropology." What is at stake here is therefore quite different from any desire to carve out a new space among the therapeutic professions in which to apply philosophy. I would even say that the acute self-reflection of psychoanalysis tends towards this step – the philosophical assumption of the search for biographically experiential meaning – almost as much as the request that makes the normal, terrifying suffering of the many explicit.

Again, this passage through depth psychologies cannot be relegated to the status of a simple antecedent. In order to return to a specific vocation, philosophy must humbly, usefully become a disciple, it must learn to integrate, then to differentiate, the tremendously rich experience that therapists of the psyche have known how to distill in their methods and theories. This is a difficult task, for within its techniques, in its method, a great subject and a fundamental problem are implicit. Psychoanalysis has brought another form of thought to the center of the individual's psychic life; this form is often called "symbolic," but I would like to define it as a "figural account," placing it beside and joining it with "discursive calculus." Discursive calculus implies thought in an action organized by procedures; it is apt for describing and rationally organizing actions, methods and perceptions, according to a determinate goal.

Of course these are only two convenient extremes for typifying (i.e. showing the dominance of a mixed union) small, infinite variations in the composition of gestures, images and thoughts. Even philosophy has come to terms with the various forms of "figural accounts," sometimes valorizing them, sometimes judging them inferior. The relation between myth and logos is one of the most frequent commonplaces in philosophical debates. Art and, in part, religion's questions and attempts at understanding certainly have much to teach every hermeneutist and analyst about the oneiric, imaginative and even symptomatic manifestations of psychic life.

What marks psychoanalytic innovation, however, is the fact that we need to take this path in order to understand the emotional, affective totality of the motivations of psychic life, even when they appear purely reasonable. Rationality, at least in lived life, must deal with a territory of forces which remain hidden from it, for they speak in a different, often alien, language. Only careful discernment can separate what is on the defensive with respect to something that we cannot or do not want to accept in ourselves and about ourselves, from what compensates for undervalued weaknesses. Or again, from what we ideologically use to justify secretly the "here and now" with an appeal to custom; from what, finally, expresses a biographical circumstance gleaned from the deep. It is therefore a necessary catharsis for being able to take our own thought seriously, when it involves questions that concern us intensely and personally.

Psychoanalysis's second important innovation is that it questions the relationship that discourse (any discourse, even a discourse on physics) has with lived biographical elements. But we must be careful here: I am not making a claim about reducing thought to psychological subjectivity, but rather attempting to take in this perspective, to be able to observe this dimension *as well*. Therefore, if we wish to retrieve a possible trajectory of meaning, and if we see the need for a "biographical path" in this trajectory, then we must learn to integrate into philosophical practice the psychoanalytic stance that valorizes and investigates the forms of figural account as a preferential mode of access to deep psychic life and to its importance for biography.

In short, the philosopher must put himself at risk, he must engage in his discipline knowing that his life really is "at stake." Nevertheless, he must be able to see when he has to send people with full-fledged psychopathologies into proper care. Biographical philosophy can be the search for meaning that it wishes to be if it is aware that one of its necessary preconditions is that we be in a "relatively normal" psychological state, one that allows us to have "relatively good," important affective relations, and to work, to participate in the shared world's functions and institutions.

Psychoanalysis too would gain by having a tight relation with philosophy. The widespread belief that the psychoanalyst can, and must, be neutral – in the particular sense of not introducing his or her own private convictions into the therapy, while still maintaining the sense of neutrality that consists in not using the relations with his or her patients to satisfy his or her own affective needs – is too simplified a shortcut. For the moment, I will leave aside the correspondences that this position maintained in order to follow the medical model, in order to legitimate psychoanalysis as a science, and in order to free the analyst from the intricate nexus of reciprocal interdependence with his or her patients.

Yet, in another way, neutrality means protecting the analyst and patient from slipping into religious, political or philosophical indoctrination. This position was originally justified by Freud, who did not leave it as a technical warning. But Freud could certainly engage in this form of neutrality, because it fully clarified his world-view, claiming to adhere perfectly to the "scientific conception of the world."

Even in his own time, Freud's massive assertion ought to have solicited a more complex development that explained the precise connections binding "science" – and which "science," anyway? – to psychoanalytic procedures; today, claiming that there is a pure coincidence between psychoanalysis and science is rather delicate. And what would the "scientific conception of the world" be? In what sense can a conception of the world be scientific? Merely by asking the question, are we not already fully in the domain of philosophy, indeed of "metaphysics," given that when we speak of a conception of the world, we imply a totality? Perhaps then we mean the "scientific method"? And the scientific method along epistemological lines? Then should we speak more specifically about the philosophy of science or of knowledge? And if so, then *which* philosophy of science or of knowledge? Are we talking only about science as a consensus about publicly verifiable results? Then questions about the type of dependability one can expect from reports that are based on "clinical case" histories, and about verifiability and falsification, would be inevitable. And again, can we assimilate the different methods proper to different sciences without further specification? Finally: can psychoanalysis be assimilated to other scientific practices, and if not, then what particular feature allows it to belong to the family of sciences while still keeping it distinct from the others?

Barricading oneself within the fantasmatic walls of the "scientific conception of the world," or claiming to demonstrate that psychoanalysis can exhibit methods and results that are comparable to what is done in other scientific sectors seems unreasonable to me, and fundamentally disrespectful of the technical innovations, methods and concepts that have been made available by a rich psychoanalytical practice that is now centuries old.

I believe that the most precise neutrality consists in being aware that one's own conception of the world nevertheless influences any selection of the clinical material that one uses in order to encourage the patient to come to terms with it. Again, there is an unconscious philosophy at work even in the attention to somato-psychic reactions that the relation and its transfer and countertransfer processes cause. And inevitably we activate our whole personality, including its whole identity, when we move on to describing and interpreting a trajectory. We need not engage in long explanations; rather, we must be conscious of knowing how to alert the other, within convenient limits, as the situation requires, when it becomes useful or necessary. This type of communication can reinforce the perception that the analyst is another person, one who is capable of a certain type of knowledge linked to his or her position in the relation; and this perception is complementary and opposed to the supposed, imaginary knowledge of an idealized analyst. In this way, we assure the appreciation and acceptance of the dimension of singularity, and a mutual feeling of belonging to a common human limit.

All the same, at work in Freudian neutrality was the conviction that pathology was the echo in the present of a past history whose memory corresponded to a possible reworking and cure that was relived in the therapeutic relation. If there is no doubt that a certain traumatic fixation exists, preventing or impoverishing a connection with the present or an image of the future, psychopathology's most decisive leverage – barring very serious cases – is precisely in the obstacle that hinders the ever-necessary construction of self in the present, and in the possible future. The present obstacle flows back towards the past in search of a history, of a probable origin. As in every occasion of life, the feeling that one has failed in the present brings with itself the whole trajectory that has led us to the point where we find ourselves in check. This bind between a boarded-up future and an unredeemable past that still seems to contain its efficient causes is the cage that imprisons us in neurosis and psychosis.

Such a method, which moreover is quite common today even in Freudian schools, brings with it the possibility of surpassing the neutral search for the causes of the unsatisfying (and too satisfying) developments of infantile libido.

If the problem is in the present-future, and flows back from there towards the past, then, within the limits of the possible, constructing the history of life, choosing one's attitude with respect to existence, becomes of capital importance. Placed in its biographical circumstantiality, the ethical interrogative becomes inevitable. And precisely for this reason it becomes irreducible to any prescription, however sensitive to the drama of conflicting values, that can generate new, creative prospects, or degenerate into coercion and destructiveness. Here the work of depth psychologies meets biographical ethics. Ever since Freud imbued psychoanalysis with the scientific spirit, it has claimed to concentrate on a sort of natural development of the libido, investigating the subject's history very meticulously, but only in as much as it reflects a steady movement from the primitive horde to modern man.

Even in this regard it would be good to be clear, given that most analysts who dedicate themselves to theorizing would relegate these theses to the history of thought, without making them their own. Yet Freud's scientific fantasies contain a double move: "nature" – i.e. the biological inheritance of the species – is reduced (for psychic and psychopathological relevance) first to sexual libido and self-preservational instincts, then to the conflict between Eros and Thanatos; at the same time, collective and individual history enters psychoanalytic observation as an obstacle to or facilitation of a natural process that tends toward psychosexual, genital organization, or towards cancelling vital tensions.

Here I would like to point out the fact that it is precisely this approach which makes it truly impossible to understand the root cause of the change in psychopathologies. Hysteria, which was the initial theory's stepping-stone, has almost "disappeared," diffusing a few symptomatic features in different psychopathological domains. If one were to write a history of psychiatry from this point of view (as has already occurred for some pathologies), one would note how nosographic categories regularly change without gaining in plausibility from within psychiatric disciplines. As a matter of principle, any consideration of that historical, socio-cultural world so breathlessly chased after is excluded from the unreflected, "naturalistic," theoretical formulation.

It is absolutely necessary to specify that the window, which is closed onto the world of psychiatric and psychoanalytic study, cannot prevent the world, with all of its changes, from entering by the same door that opens to admit the patient. Even if it is already unwittingly at work in the unreflective process of changing perception and categorization that pre-order the therapist's thoughts. Therefore we are not dealing with occasional delays, or theoretical compromises that change the representation of the intrapsychic and intersubjective. This was achieved by overlapping theory upon theory, but rarely by inserting the world and its history into theory.

It is therefore imperative that we meditate on the question of whether the ancient philosophical search, which did not sunder the soul and the world, is not in fact the root to which we must return in order to find inspiration for future methods. Not in order to have immediate answers, but in order not to avoid inevitable questions, risking that they remain unanswered. The psychoanalyst teaches the philosopher that fore-warned impotence is always better than hard-headed, inefficient declarations of grandiosity, with their unconscious backdrop of inferiority.

The exclusion of the world, or its reduction to a question of drives, has forced even research on the phylogenetic, biological conditions of the Freudian school into the too narrow parameters of infantile sexual libido; it has forced the research of the Jungian school into archetypal theory, which is still unable to distinguish accurately between hereditary coordination, orientation movement, perceptual innatism, biorhythms, models of reference and structures of preference on the one hand, and constructions of cultural imagination on the other. While attachment theories and theories of objectival and interpersonal relations individuate the constitutive structure of even the intrapsychic world, within the originally relational being, they almost exclusively prefix the relation of infantile therapy to the whole biographical, historical process. Once again, it seems to me that the isolationism of the psychic monad is mitigated by the substitution of the isolated dyad, placed at the origin of that world which instead connects its most intimate and secret moves.

The indivisibility of the soul and the world may suggest an extension of comparative research, as much in the direction of deepening the ethological constants of the human species as in that of the cultural elaborations connected to them from one time to another and from one area to another. Along these lines, I think I see how we can go beyond the assumption of atomistic individualism and uncritical ethnocentrism, which has often undermined depth psychologies and the possibility of understanding why, given different cultures and different historical periods, different psychological theories all succeed in helping psychic suffering, even though they obviously answer to generally human constants. And at the same time, this is the challenge and the epistemological opportunity offered by developments in ethno-psychiatry and ethno-psychoanalysis.

5 Mythobiography as a Therapy and as a Search for Wisdom

In order to investigate the relationship between therapy and narration we must ask what the disposition and events that cure the psyche are, and, from there, what role narration and self-narration play among them. I will further limit the domain by specifying that I will be referring to therapies of the soul – scientifically called the "psyche" – that have been used in the last century, from psychoanalytic discoveries onward. The first factor – not quite empirical, I would say *approximately* empirical – that groups the commonsense of experts in the field (at least the ones who are open to considering different psychotherapies without the excessive hesitation that stems from belonging to a particular school) is that theories and techniques, which may be quite different among themselves, reach results that are in the main not very dissimilar, in terms of subjective well-being and the significance of the experience, according to those in therapy.

At the same time, ethno-psychiatry and ethno-psychoanalysis are rooted in psychoanalytic knowledge, testifying to the fact that even practices that have been labelled by others, or in the past, as witchcraft, can in certain conditions be therapeutically effective, precisely where cultural pre-understandings of illnesses remain foreign to the techniques of modern Western psychic therapy. Thus the first step in investigating therapeutic factors is to locate what is common to very different techniques, methods and theories.

1. The feature that is common to all therapies is the relationship of trust that one must enter into in order to begin treatment. One trusts someone and entrusts oneself to him or her, confiding events and emotions that one would not talk about or show to anyone other than a "good friend." This practice reproduces some of the features of an attachment relationship,[4] inevitably accompanied by tensions regarding separation and fears of loss. We could therefore say that this relationship is mimetic of primary relationships of care in general, and of maternal relationships particularly.

2. What develops between patient and therapist is an asymmetrical relationship: the therapist in fact represents an assumed knowledge that is capable of explaining and helping to repair behaviors that are counterproductive for the patient's manner of living. This relationship too rekindles a trust, this time to another person's "greater," more experienced knowledge. The accumulation and interweaving of these first two relational positions form the juncture of potentially "remembering, repeating and working-through"[5] one's original relationship with one's parents, or with the original figures who were charged with one's care and upbringing. In other words, the therapeutic relationship in its formal presentation already establishes the condition of possibility for recrossing the relationship from which culture originates; it reactivates the social impulses inherent to primary therapies, transferring them into a changed and reflexively advantageous context.[6]

3. The therapeutic question arises from an obstacle to life perspectives, from self-understanding and from a pre-understanding that all interact with an affective order such that they reproduce one's judgement, one's feeling of being a

[4] The clear bibliographical reference is John Bowlby's fundamental text, *Attachment and Loss*.
[5] This is the title of a famous essay of Freud's, "Remembering, repeating and working-through."
[6] Both the expression "social instincts" as well as the ideas associated with it come from Irenäus Eibl-Eibesfeldt.

subject who is inept at confronting present experiences, future possibilities and the meaning of one's own past. Different psychotherapeutic techniques tend to depend upon available conscious and unconscious resources in order to reshape a personality's behavior that is capable of relating to others and to the world in the most satisfying way possible, surpassing the "obstacle" of being able to "have an experience." In using a metaphor that carries great weight for anthropology and psychology, I could perhaps say that different therapeutic techniques seek to facilitate the formation of a new center for the personality.

4. Every transformation needs to transmit movement to an unsatisfying though crystallized, if not ossified, order. Through very different processes, psychotherapies recombine time, revisiting the past and making it current again, such that the present and the image of the future are influenced and modified by it. In any case, the framework and rhythm of time tend to move, following perspectives that are made possible by the act of reliving and reflecting. The same interpretation acts as an opening to temporalities that are different from the fixity that is taken for granted and that has encysted itself in the repetition of erroneous self-knowledge. It is in the figure of time that the function of autobiographical and biographical narration and re-narration fully emerge in therapy, precisely because the spirit of narration possesses, as Thomas Mann said, a certain measure of power over time.

5. From a space that is both protected from every obligation to act and immediately reply, and freed in the presence of a seemingly unconditioned, affective recognition, the effect of putting one's own self-representation back into play prepares the way for a new symbolism, for the fusion of image, affection and thought in a different figure of meaning, where meaning is vital, biographical orientation.

Different therapeutic techniques merely recreate the conditions for displaying the eminently human faculty of creative imagination, of imagining differently. Man is a visionary animal before he is anything else: in as much as every human faculty is specifically human, it is in fact involved in the potential to transform any given into another, beginning by imagining it differently. This is an eminent distinction, and at the same time a supreme danger. Required attention is postulated in delimiting the space and time of therapy, and in its conscious address to the obstacles to realization, comprehension and acceptance, placed by the effectual immersion of lived biographical elements into history.

Imagining things differently requires a certain level of de-automatization of emotional feeling, perception and thought, which must be considered carefully. There are many, many ways to favor the nascent state of imagination and its symbolic evolution, which, nevertheless, is never born with a clean slate: one's reactivated imaginative capacity inevitably develops possible symbolic combinations, beginning from cultural models that have moulded each individual's understanding of himself and the world. Biography then measures itself against mythemes that are part of its heredity,[7] and imagination looks for new ways to formulate it that can answer the present's questions, assuring a link with the roots of culture. Every innovation, even every overturning, is an implicit recognition of the necessary relationship with the originary humus. It is this dynamic whole that I call "mythobiography."

6. However flexible a personality is, any therapy finally tends to establish communication among psychic divisions, and to facilitate an articulation presenting its unity, as the psychic equivalent of the biological organism's unity and of the question of the individual's responsibility that his or her cultural community poses.

I write these words on care for the soul with circumspection and respect, the more so as they need to be preserved (almost hidden?) from the necessary consumption that wreaks havoc upon us, and that arises from the fashions of the market and culture, but also from the controlled administration of people's "desire for health" – with all the welcome assonances and similes that the expression "desire for health" manages to elicit. These are the circumspection and respect that one owes to the things of "divine service," understood in a sense that is so large, so syncretic (indeed, unabashedly ecumenical) that no religious therapy for the soul, and no psychoanalytic therapy, has had until now. "Taking care" of the soul is in fact a big word, and perhaps for this reason it is fenced in

---

[7] The term "mythobiography" comes from Ernst Bernhard.

by the proprieties of faith, theories or schools. Paradoxically – though not at all for anyone familiar with Jung –[8] it is precisely in the possible ecumenism of theories that I sense how much of my Jungian education is still worth holding on to (beyond the theory of the process of individuation, the conception of thinking with symbols and the importance of compensating for interpretation).

By "biographical ecumenism" I do not mean an improbable jumble of techniques and theories. I am thinking rather of a theory and technique that are able to order any contribution around the selective, circumstantial and unifying criterion of what they are treating. Or the criterion of anything that can care for the particular developing biography which admits its stalemate, with me and before me, and which at least partially rewrites the stories that until that moment it had considered representative of itself. The most determined, unrepeatable individuality is in fact the most universal concept, end and instrument: we are in fact *all* unrepeatable individuals. This allows experiential contents and more disparate cultural scenarios to agree in unity in order to realize a story (or biography) that can withstand the bumps, tears and back-peddling of existence. The ordering desire of analysis is to recognize ourselves in a personal myth that finds new developments in our own life story.

What I have described above is inconceivable without the obstructed perspective that is enclosed in a prescribed, malevolent meaning being corrupted and made only one possible perspective. I thereby intend to go beyond anti-identitary rhetoric. The fixity of identity is obviously a historical construct made obsolete by the developments of global capitalism and the culture of the crisis of modernity. And one can perceive an obsessive defense mechanism at work in identitary preoccupations, but one's ability to maintain the unitary nexus in self-narration remains the condition for any comparison with oneself and the world, wherever the subject wanders and however it is annihilated. Thus, in the concept and method of biography and mythobiography, the theory

---

[8] The same denomination of the Jungian school as "analytical psychology" was meant to express, according to Jung's intentions, the unity of the analytical and therapeutic field that took up Freudian and Adlerian orientation in addition to the orientation of "complex psychology," a term that better described the Jungian specific.

and practice of therapy and of the search for meaning formulate an alternative both to identifying in identitary fixities, and to the fragmenting dispersal of postmodern ideology.

Having said this, it is no coincidence that all theories, with hundreds of variations, tend to push the imagination and its symbolic potentialities. There are labyrinths in life where we will get lost, or be eaten by monsters, if we are unable to "imagine differently." I believe this is the fundamental distinction, not in absolute terms, but as regards quality and extension,[9] which makes culture the specific quality of our species. And, whether we know it or not, every technique that carefully considers desires, fantasies, dreams, thought experiments, transferences, interpretations, games, drawings or whatever else active imaginations can produce (i.e. that is developed by individuals and not reproduced from the avalanche of symbols proposed by the media) invokes this fundamental anthropic capacity.

Nevertheless, that which makes sure that it is possible, within and beyond the pathology's therapy, to take care of the meaning of a life, cannot leave the reconstruction of the link and the re-activation of symbolic capacities in isolation: care for meaning occurs where the events that the analytic encounter calls forth are grouped into a particular narration that traces a path, i.e. in a narration, which recounts the events of the search for meaning, and which, by narrating them, unveils that meaning.

Schematically, I would say that during a course of therapy, but often in the course of a single sitting, four modes of narration intertwine: a) fragments of one's life story; b) descriptions of the context constituted by the cultural configuration that has influenced family events; c) conversations between analyst and patient; d) references to symbolic images which are woven together and transformed by subjective experience, and which point to a possible mythobiography.

In mythobiographical narration the conjunction between symbolic image and subjective lived experience expresses a great deal of emotion and invites a lively curiosity for research, but it also gravitates towards the structure of nar-

---

[9] For an overview of the "culture" of non-human animals, see Franz M. Wuketits.

ration itself and the decisive moments of its intrigue. By "structure of narration" I mean that the organization of space and time is of paramount importance in mythobiography: in other words, the search for the "center" and the quality of impression on memory that we designate by whatever has an indefinite, nearly eternal, duration. The image's power imposes itself then as "kratophany," and as such can reach the feeling of sacred experience and evoke its thought.[10]

At the same time it is characteristic of rites and myths that they organize their multiform appearance around the image of the center, of duration and of the imposition of a power that is external to the ego that experiences it: this way of narrating, or better of *re-narrating*, characterizes itself by hosting the event of meaning. Meaning in fact establishes the direction of experience and its projectuality, and the direction comes from the centering of space, from the duration of time, and from the energy that sets the impulse and rhythm of movement.

But the fact that myth is so singularly linked to the word "biography" is something that only modernity can explain. The pre-modern norm that informs every institution, including the psychology of individuals, dictates that we assimilate ourselves as much as possible to exemplary conduct, that we follow the model. The opposite of the norm, which has gradually become victorious in the course of modernity, dictates instead that we seek out novelty and originality, even when we take our inspiration from tradition.[11]

History must therefore translate itself into histories, and these latter into biographies. It would seem as if nothing could stop the dissemination of histories. Yet this would be an unhappy plurality of difference, firstly because, outside of their common feature of being different, they would cease to be so; they would become such incomparable singularities that they would return to the unrelated unity of identity and, necessarily in the end, to the aphasia of an identity that is fleeting unto itself. Secondly because, in the end, nothing is more universal than individuality, whose history is precisely biography: the individ-

[10] On the relation between meaning and the sacred, see Armido Rizzi.
[11] On the relation between subject and individual in the history of philosophy, see Christoph Riedel. On the relation between individual and society from a sociological and philosophical point of view, see Jürgen Ritsert.

ual as such is in fact the universal that houses different ethno-linguistic, class and gender distinctions.[12]

The mark of greatness of a century of psychoanalysis and biographical and autobiographical methods[13] is precisely its religious attention at the borders of grand history, and its patient excavation among the details and leftovers of identitary monumentalities. And it is precisely in this apparently infinite drift of fragmentary irrelevancies that revisiting myth is triggered. And with it, the possibility of re-opening the centering of meaning, by inscribing it, however singularly, within grand history and the durable process of the cosmos – as Novalis predicted when he wrote that each person's life is his or her Bible, or will become his or her Bible. And this triggering does not occur by suggestive influences, nor by chance; I think rather that we must see an anthropological necessity in the reference and transforming assumption that biography performs upon myth, translated into a form that is adapted to the cultural configuration of modernity and its crisis.

In the different forms of therapeutic narration, we have seen the event of meaning specifically delineate itself in response to an avowal of disorientation and lack of motivation. Therapeutic narration here encounters the search for wisdom. Specifically that search for wisdom which we must, in Western terminology, call "philosophy," if it does not immediately coincide with a set of beliefs and acts that need to be performed according to a greater-than-human revelation, i.e. if it does not immediately coincide with adherence to a religion.

Of course I mean a philosophy that does not limit itself to the usual practices of professors and students of philosophy, who usually read, comment on and interpret texts with the aim of clarifying concepts that are already in use, and of formulating more adequate ones. But even the use of the word "philoso-

---

[12] On individualization as a process that is peculiar to second modernity (or reflexive modernity), see in particular Ulrich Beck, in Paul Heelas, Scott Lash and Paul Morris. For a socio-anthropological view, see Norbert Elias, and Michael Carrithers, Steven Collins and Steven Lukes.
[13] On biography and autobiography, see the works of Duccio Demetrio. On the diary as technique, see Ira Progoff.

phy" that I propose here should not sound new or current. To this effect, I quote Pierre Hadot, one of the most admired living experts on classical philosophy:

> Under the influence of Bergson, and then of existentialism, I have always understood philosophy as a total transformation of our way of seeing the world and of being in it. I had not foreseen [...] that I would spend my life studying ancient thought, and more particularly the influence that Greek philosophy had on Latin literature. Yet the mysterious conjunction of chance and inner necessity that forms our destinies oriented me in this direction. In my studies I saw that many of the difficulties we encounter when trying to understand ancient philosophical works often come from the fact that we commit a double anachronism in interpreting them: we think that, like many modern works, they are meant to communicate information regarding a given conceptual content, and that we can also directly extract clear details from them about their author's thought and psychology. But very often in fact they are spiritual exercises that the author himself performs and has his reader perform. They are meant to form souls. They have a psychogogical value.[14]

Here it is well, if only summarily, to differentiate this way of understanding philosophy, as a "philosophical practice" in the search for wisdom, from both psychotherapy and a renewal of ancient schools of wisdom.

To begin with, psychopathology is not the point of interest and the need that must be addressed when considering psychotherapies: what philosophical practice must take care of is life in its normality, and thence, life in the precariousness of its meaning and its unawareness of this precariousness. That is, of course, if we follow the Socratic conviction that the most worthy life is dedicated to the search for meaning. Not having psychopathological symptomatologies as its central interest, philosophical practice is not an activity, much less an attitude that can claim to be finished once it has reached a certain result: it is rather a path to life.

---

[14] Pierre Hadot (1981), p. 9. [This foreword is not reproduced in the English translation of the book – *Translator's note*.] It is interesting to note that a later work of Hadot's (2002), is a biographical interview whose philosophical theme is the intertwining of thought and life experience.

Finally, analytical "neutrality" can be maintained in order to keep the therapist from mediating the choices and daily life of the other person, thus facilitating the possibility of entering into a relationship in all of the various roles that transference assigns, but it must abandon the obscurity of its references with regard to the philosophical position of whoever offers him or herself as a guide.

I cannot adequately discuss here what problems this sort of clarification represents in the relationship: in fact the solution to the conflict between service to the other person's growth towards freedom, and towards his or her conscious individualization on the one hand, and the guide's explicit epistemological and ethical position on the other, depends upon the philosophies that one adheres to. Of course we cannot avoid answering such an important question; the usefulness of every proposal of philosophical practice depends upon the answer that one provides. In other words, we need a philosophy that is capable of serving the other's freedom and individuality without forcing us to renounce our convictions.

I would moreover like to point out, without prevaricating, that my proposal of biographical philosophy*[15]* in fact represents a possible solution to the tension between announcing one's own philosophical point of view and service to the other's free search for meaning.

Let me finally say a few words about the difference between the ancient schools and the philosophical practice that I am indicating. The difference I referred to earlier, between emulating a model and the process of individuation, between insertion into a myth and mythobiography, still obtains. In addition to this fundamental conceptual difference, and in order to differentiate the philosophical practice as it is understood here from modern and contemporary philosophical methods, I will list the sources of mine that must be sifted, selected and integrated in a renewed philosophical practice: a) the philosophical tradition; b) techniques of meditation; c) the biographical and autobiographical methods; d) psychological processes; e) the rules of communication that center

---

[15] By "my proposal" I am also of course referring to Luigi Vero Tarca's essay in this book. Differences in training, language and formulation in fact enrich the design of an authentically universal and individual philosophy and individual and universal biographicity.

around biography and that are able to enlarge one's perspective and suggest alternate ones without excluding the subjective truth of the participants in a dialogue.

⑥ "Longing-Law" and Its Pathologies

"Sacrifice" is a word that has been in decline for nearly half a century in the cultural lexicon and implicit psychology of those countries at the center of the global economy. After the efforts at reconstruction following World War Two, the ideology and reality of the production of consumer goods, the increase in social spending, the displacement of armed conflict towards the edges of the world, and the transformation of the idea of war between Western and Eastern blocks into that of nuclear war (with its corollary of the irrelevance of sacrifice on the part of the civilian and fighting populations) have made the teaching of sacrifice obsolete. For thousands of years, and for all socio-economic systems that were based on a scarcity of goods for the ruled, this teaching had constituted the meaning of the transmission of knowledge from one generation to the next.

Looking at it from a non-Western perspective, one might think that what was in question was a result of having exported the weight of life as sacrifice from the countries at the center of the capitalist system to the edges, which the bad conscience of the world's rulers have named "developing nations," with its promise of false hope. More explicitly: it served economic expansion on Henry Ford's model; it served to create a wide social consensus against the communist threat, and to legitimize hegemonic policies with respect to the Third World; it created a type of human mass bent on consuming as much as possible, convinced that it lived in a world whose future was guaranteed by progress, and which, therefore, had abolished the need for self-sacrifice and the need to teach the value of sacrifice to its own children.[16] It is this transforma-

---

[16] The false echo of the term "sacrifice" is terrible and pathetic each time that calls to war resound, even in countries at the heart of the global system: terrible because a devastating power is

tion that has brought worldly asceticism, which had been the spirit of capitalism of the preceding centuries, to the "longing-law" [*licitazionismo*] of global capitalism, which in part coincides with the cultural features that we call "postmodern."

"Longing-law" is a term that I have taken from the fifth canto of Dante's *Inferno*. There Dante describes the punishments of carnal sinners, and defines the lustful as "subjecting reason to the rule of lust," and adds that the queen Semiramis "made license licit in her laws."[17] Even the revolt against affluent capitalism in the West in the 1960s and 70s unconsciously followed the spirit of the times when it rose up, claiming that it was "forbidden to forbid." Dominant ideology has therefore abandoned the sacrifice that is characteristic of worldly asceticism (and by this term I mean "freed from the otherworldly prospect of a reward in the afterlife") as an ideal and obsolete practice, which its opponents dismissed as a falsifying cover. In its place new altars, or, better, "theaters," have arisen, which are at once dedicated to the principle of performance[18] where it concerns professions and roles, to spectacularization[19] in matters of consumption, and to one's relationship to others and to egotism, i.e. to the cult of the ego with respect to oneself. I call this group of characteristics "longing-law," a cultural configuration that deifies desire and turns it into a "law."

I believe this is the reason behind the change in the specific gravity of different psychopathologies. To schematize: if symptomatic hysteria is seen as the expression of a drive, and an aspiration towards relationships excluded from legitimation, and if, at the other extreme of the psychoneurotic spectrum, clini-

---

evoked, recalled from the realm of repressed myths and now stripped of all the precautions that traditionally and ritually accompanied it; pathetic because the call to sacrifice is immediately followed by the reassurance that the war will be over very soon, and will be fought from a very safe distance, i.e. with a host of measures that reveal the total absence of a spirit of sacrifice on the part of the populace. Governments know that it was the black bags containing the bodies of the marines who died in Vietnam, and the "enemy," that defeated the United States, and therefore those bags must not be seen again. In order to avoid denials, we make sure that neither bodies nor funerals of soldiers killed in combat are "seen" any longer.

[17] Dante Alighieri, canto V, lines 39, 56.

[18] On the principle of performance, see Herbert Marcuse.

[19] I have obviously taken this term from Guy Debord.

cal obsession is interpreted as the law's defensive overinvestment against drives and relational models that could threaten it, the whole horizon changes when desire itself is proclaimed law.

Pathologies linked to the conflict between law and desire become marginal, while the difficulty of taking and giving limits and forms to oneself becomes central, and with it the ability to constitute oneself as a relatively independent self, which is both subject and object of the interrelation. Pathologies of the self, personality disorders, borderline typologies, as well as eating disorders, depression and mania are registering an increased vulnerability in one's capacity to constitute oneself in differentiation, as much horizontally – with respect to others – as vertically – in relation to the idea and evaluation of the self.

One might suspect that today the difficult, gradual distinction and interrelation among need, desire and law would be blown apart by an uncertain storm that satisfies need, injecting it with allusions of desire, which it proposes as models of conformity, thus as exponents of the law. On the other hand, when the law reappears as limit and is left to desire, it loses its sense of a symbolic order, and must impose itself in a mere clash, as the "reality" of strength alone, i.e. stripped of any authentic authority, unable to legitimize itself beyond the fact that it "obtains."

Need can in fact be understood as the sign of a lack in the object, as much in relation to the perceivable world as to internal experience. Need is therefore determined by its object; desire, on the other hand, feels a lack that is paradoxically defined by the indeterminate evocation of referrals that it elicits around and inside any one of its objects.

We could therefore say that production is the need of our civilization, built as it is on the dynamic center of economic accumulation: the exchange and consumption of goods that are destined for profit through production, the exchange and consumption of infinite, protean solicitations of desire.

Desire is produced because it is only by producing desire that we can profitably sell and consume the limitless ocean of sensitive and supersensitive goods which make our historical situation possible.

In this movement we can see the theophany of our true god, the one who willingly or not presides over our *ultimate concern*, as Tillich called man's particular orientation towards the sacred. This god who dominates us is in fact money, which exists to increase itself, as per the definition of capital.

Capital is fundamentally desiring, for fundamentally there is never enough, or, when there is too much to continue increasing, it ceases being capital and destroys itself in crises. Nevertheless, capital lacks nothing to take god's place, a place that doubtless belongs to it in our world. The unquenchable thirst it elicits is the effect of the impossibility of saturating its infinitely stretched dynamics, i.e. stretched to that bad infinity that has no infinite within which to contain itself. And this is perhaps similar to the wind that never rests, pushing the lustful towards infernal punishment in Dante's canto.

Capital is truly a different god from those that were worshipped in every pre-modern culture; different too from the god that accompanied the preceding phases of historic capitalism.

The difference between the divine and human worlds was marked precisely by the limitation of desire, by its renunciation even, by sacrifice (by disinterested offering) as a stage towards the dimension of what lasts, of what is the center and power, to the hierophanic dimension, which is proper to the appearance of the sacred. If one does not sacrifice the desire for what changes and disappears, for what turns around something else, for what can be shaken, then the sacred remains out of reach. The supreme desire – the desire to reach the astral dimension which remains veiled and which has inspired the name "desire" – is the end of desire, both in the sense of its removal – its being already satisfied, and therefore no longer existing – and in the sense of it beginning to be removed, in the practice that symbolizes and anticipates the end of desire, in sacrifice.

In reality every desire is improper: it cannot contain itself. Loyalty to the desiring power means renouncing every desire. This paradoxical dialectic is well-known even to such paths as Hinduism and Buddhism, which recognize the root of suffering in consenting to desire. And quite obviously so, for even freedom must in some way be desired, and being able to reach even the lack of desire for freedom again paradoxically represents a perfectly sublimated form of desire.

In any case, either every determinable desire must be overcome through loyalty to its excess – as in the Judeo-Christian-Islamic examples –[20] or desiring something for itself must be sacrificed, and every desire abandoned, through the recognition of the root of suffering.[21] I must stress that neither "God" nor "emptiness" should here be understood as "something;" they are in fact different from anything that can be conceived of as a thing. Viewed from this summit, the paths of desire and non-desire meet, and together they signal their distance from the meaning, however common and good, that is proper to our civilization. The god of economic accumulation reigns at its center, and the ego that sees itself in every identification and projection as its human appendage (sensor of production, exchange and consumption) is its necessary complement.

7 Sacrifice of the Ego

The ancient figure of the saint, as well as that of the sage, is almost always an ascetic figure whose efforts to reach knowledge and virtue occupy the entire field of life. And in asceticism he distances himself from subjection to the vanity of a life that is unexamined and bent to the twisted habit of denial, or of negation, or of the repression of its worrying, interrogative essence.

Precisely for this sacrificial aspect, cultures of scarcity highly esteemed those who, through a life dedicated to spirituality, exempted[22] themselves from the obligations of procreation and family on the one hand, or from work on the

---

[20] One example of extreme Hasidic simplicity might be the following: "The Greatest Lust. A learned man once said to the rabbi of Rozdol: 'It seems to me that the condition of being a zaddik is the greatest of all lusts.' 'That's how it is,' the rabbi replied, 'but to attain to it, you first have to get the better of all the lesser lusts.'" Martin Buber, (1949), p. 219.

[21] Obviously this is purely schematic: in both Hindu and Buddhist Tantrism desire is welcomed and transformed. An exemplary text is Abhinava Ghupta's *Tantraloka*.

[22] I owe the concept of exoneration to Arnold Gehlen.

other, but who in any case refused to justify themselves on the basis of immediate social utility. And today all of them would be deemed useless according to the pervasive modern perspective.

One might even think, anthropologically, that in exonerating such individuals from many, or from some, of the commonly accepted tasks of profane life, these cultures venerated the fundamental cultural gap, i.e. the specifically human position that defers an immediate reply to internal drives and external stimuli in order to reflect upon and rework them into actions that are at least partially free from ambient and physio-psychic influence. Here I must stress that reflection does not yet imply mental representations that are clearly distinguishable from techniques (whether material or spiritual, to use an approximate, and in many ways anachronistic, terminology) that have been put to work on external nature and one's own corporeality.

The human capacity to exist in this gap (most of all, to grow up completely in it) is obviously conditioned by phylogenetic particularities working amongst themselves; for example, upright stature, freedom for the hand to manipulate and subjugate its surroundings, corticalization and cerebral differentiation, the development of language. These conditions, *if taken altogether in their interworkings*, make it possible *to imagine differently*, to invent cultures. Thus by venerating the figure of one who shirks the dictates of need and worldly desires, cultures have unconsciously venerated their act of birth, man's specific difference. And this is an originary condition of a culture that finds itself raised into a suspension of influences of the external and internal worlds, which is proper to spiritual practices.

In these practices, sacrifice moves towards the inside, it becomes internalized. One formidable example is psalm 51 (according to the numbering of the Massoretic text), also known as the *Miserere*, which reads (verses 16-17):

Quoniam si voluisses sacrificium, dedissem utique: holocaustis non delectaberis / Sacrificium Deo spiritus contribulatus: cor contritum, et humiliatum, Deus, non despicies

or, in the King James version:

For thou desirest not sacrifice; else would I give it: thou delightest not in burnt offering. The sacrifices of God are a broken spirit: a broken and a contrite heart, O God, thou wilt not despise.

Here the "productive" *ruah* – which in Hebrew means a female spirit that is an efficient power in God – is a human attitude that is aware of "sin," and is therefore broken and humbled. But Jewish "sin" leads to *hatà*, which means "to lose one's way, not to arrive where one was meant to arrive," or to *avon*, which means "to move further from one's objective."[23] Both of these terms recur in the *Miserere*, as do other terms that refer to guilt and sin. Thus the spirit that is aware of its inadequacy, its lacunas, its inability and impotence becomes a willing "sacrifice." This attitude suspends its own judgement, it no longer puts itself into the care of its need, it does not immediately attempt to realize its desire, which through a pun in Hebrew becomes the lust to fill its maw. (The lustful root of *avon* is linked with the soul-throat-*nephesh*.) This attitude is far from the immediacy of orality, the most obvious symbol, because it is the source of the undeferrability of need, of the intolerability of frustration.

This miniscule extension of the theme of the internalization of sacrifice[24] allows us to shift our attention to the meaning that the analytical encounter, right from its first session, has historically and inevitably carried with it in the context of a civilization that fundamentally disdains sacrifice. In fact, the first rule when stipulating a contract between analyst and patient involves ascertaining one's ability to tolerate frustration: if one is unable to linger in the gap that develops between need and the suspension of the search for satisfaction, one cannot experience the lack that constitutes the essence of desire, and therefore a favorable place will not materialize, one which could contain a search for knowledge that listens to the psyche (which in its essence is a search for mean-

---

[23] R. Della Rocca, p. 12.

[24] The God of Israel prefers the "sacrifice of praise" (*Psalms* 50:14), i.e. the "calves of our lips" (*Hosea* 14:2), to the sacrifice of holocausts, for it is there that the limit of orality turns into the creation and offering of words.

ing, and therefore the necessary psychological correlative of every philosophical practice), and that is able to foster the personality's transformation. The resonance with the productive gap of every human culture here comes to the fore, the original gap that suspends the profusion of external stimuli and internal drives. At the root of more general theoretical consequences, both in Freudian and Jungian thought, is this elementary first step of any analytical process, which is common to all schools and tendencies.

The following affirmation by Freud has now almost taken on the proportions of a saying:

> In the course of centuries the *naïve* self-love of men has had to submit to two major blows at the hands of science. The first was when they learnt that our earth was not the centre of the universe.... The second blow fell when biological research destroyed man's supposedly privileged place in creation.... [i.e. Copernicus and Darwin] But human megalomania will have suffered its third and most wounding blow from the psychological research of the present time which seeks to prove to the ego that it is not even master in its own house, but must content itself with scanty information of what is going on unconsciously in its mind.[25]

"*Naïve* self-love" and "human megalomania" are names for psycho-cultural resistance to psychoanalysis that express aspects of what Freud called "narcissism," a year before the lessons in his *Introductory Lectures*.

It appears clear therefore that no psychoanalytical process can take place without discerning and moving beyond certain narcissistic elements. Indeed, Clementina Pavoni forcefully claims that, "Psychoanalysis imposes a stern discipline of mortification."[26] This is one reason why we cannot avoid precedents: the modern science that Freud invokes – naturally taking into account the different modalities that modern culture offers – inevitably continues what the ancient religious and philosophical paths for the search for wisdom have always indicated as the condition for authentic knowledge. To take a source for the ancient West's way of thinking, one need only recall Plato's *Phaedo*, which

[25] Freud, (1916-1917), pp. 284-285.
[26] Silvia Lagorio, Clementina Pavoni, p. 87.

links meditation on death and death itself to philosophical art. Or at least, this is so if we understand the Platonic assertion in its quite probable sense of "spiritual exercise," which was then adopted with numerous variations by almost all of the ancient philosophical schools as the practice of being aware of life's precariousness, as attention for the present, and most of all, as an invitation to "go beyond oneself."[27]

This is not the place to enquire into the different meanings that the expression "go beyond oneself" has had in pre-capitalist culture and in global postmodern capitalism; it suffices to point to its direction: if, for the ancients, surpassing oneself was oriented toward bringing oneself closer to the *exemplary* life of sages and saints, for the moderns the same expression alludes to renouncing the ego's pseudo-omnipotent, autarchic claims. Nevertheless, I think that beyond this differentiation we ought to recognize that the same intention and dedication persist. It was precisely this persistence that Jung investigated, turning it into an archetypal element of the process of individuation, in which conscious sacrifice of the ego is the condition for recognizing the center of a renewed psychic life in the Self.

I do not agree with the historical, cultural differentiation of the modern "process of individuation," which shapes the individual on an exemplary model, and which is characteristic of pre-capitalist societies, for I believe it is not enough. At the same time, we must recognize the need to articulate, as Jung has done, the drama of sacrifice and its psychological importance for modern man against the backdrop of the great philosophical, religious tapestry that conditions its expressions. In any case, Jung was able to diagnose a figure of the egotic epidemic of our world:

> However, accentuation of the ego personality and the world of consciousness may easily assume such proportions that the figures of the unconscious are psychologized and the *self consequently becomes assimilated to the ego.*[28]

---

[27] On all of these questions concerning ancient philosophy, see the works of Pierre Hadot.
[28] C.G. Jung, 1959, vol. 9, part 2, p. 25.

I would like to underline the word "psychologized," which here more or less means, "attributed to the ego's psychic availability," and which, understood in this way, expresses a clear diagnosis of the function that "psychologization," as a surrogate of every intellectual and spiritual life, has taken on in the education and culture of the masses in countries at the heart of capitalism.

The opposite side, according to Jungian terminology, becomes bloated, cancelling the ego and its ability to discern time, space and forces, with the result that we are shaken up and sucked into absolute dimensions: the assimilation of the ego into the Self therefore leads to an improper sacralization, by which the ego's experience becomes "numinous." And this sacredness is idolatrous, or at least that is how we could translate it in theological terms. It exactly marks the border between mystic experience, which is always alive to daily realities, to the point that it favors a markedly empirical "realism,"[29] and psychotic psychopathology, which is prey to "absolutization" and to unwarranted sacralization.

Our culture however is constantly on its guard with respect to the clear possibility of psychosis, even if it is often inadequate with regard to identifying, preventing and rehabilitating etiologies. Risk takes up the unfurnished side, which is so unfurnished that it makes one think that the opposite pathology is somehow being normalized. And risk thereby takes it as a normative ideal, unleashing unpleasant feelings of inadequacy[30] with respect to obsessive maniacal behavior, which is proposed as the idealization of the "productivity" of people and things. And it would hardly be surprising if an epidemic of depression should follow, all the more because the social tie (which is the first condition and necessity of every form of human survival) is continually subjected to the blows of ferocious competition, thus favoring "protective" fusionality and individual protests of flight into the isolationist refuges of the mind and of behavior.

---

[29] Max Weber pointed out the mystic's greater sense of realism with respect to the dialectical thinker, for the former is always attentive to and respectful of the experience of "how things stand," while the latter is turned toward transformative tendencies, and for this reason is at times inclined to see them already at work even before he is able to experiment on them.
[30] See Alain Ehrenberg.

Sacrifice is therefore something very dangerous, and equally necessary: through it, the powers of creative imagination come to the fore, along with the attempt to discipline them institutionally. The powers of creative imagination celebrate their transmuting force in sacrifice: they make an effective, sacramental epiphany out of an animal, a gesture, a word, out of what has lasted beyond the lifetime of peoples and individuals, out of what is central and orients the spaces of existence, out of what contains the capacity to realize this duration and orientation. In a word, sacrifice effectuates the sacred as what stabilizes and gives direction to the time and space of life, thus as what gives meaning, thereby offering the strength of life. But for the same reasons that make this power creative, it is equally capable of destruction. If we are not able to preserve it and hand it down, it abandons us in the face of destruction; it overwhelms and annihilates individuals and communities if they do not respect the distances that they defend from every identification that cancels the profane world in the sacred, and the sacred world in the profane. In psychological terms: sacrifice cancels the ego in the "unconscious," or it assimilates it to the Self, and it assimilates the "unconscious," or the Self, to the ego.

The powers of creative imagination must therefore be disciplined; for this reason sacrifice has always been an "institution," i.e. a network of established and normative reciprocal actions.[31]

This does not mean that institutional limits are enough to prevent sacrificial idolatry; rather they are a guarantee against the possibility of the imagination flooding if it is unleashed from any destination that is measured against the vital needs of the individual and the collectivity.

If the culture of sacrifice is disappearing today, i.e. if it devalues the teaching of sacrifice within institutional boundaries, this process implies a hypertrophying of egoic features and a chain of undesired collateral effects which, at the other extreme, dismantle the sense of proportion (the *ratio*) which alone gives form to the ego. All the same, one need only look to the past, or to what impotently and violently tries to make itself felt and employs an imaginary past

---

[31] On the question of institutions, see the works of Arnold Gehlen.

in order to compete with the dominant nucleus of global capitalism (I mean of course any ideological fundamentalism based on ethnicity or religion), or in order to become aware that even the institution of sacrifice, which is logically linked to the vital direction of its powers, contains within itself the possibility of radical perversion.

The criterion of differentiation is simple: sacrificial victims do not represent a "loss" of something precious for the one who sacrifices; they represent rather the destruction of something from which one wishes to free oneself. And this is true even when the cost of slaughtering one's enemy is the loss of one's own life, as in the case of suicide attacks: here too sacrificing oneself is instrumental in the destruction of the hated other, who is the key part of the victim that must be destroyed.

There is nothing strange or unheard of in this if one considers just how much destructiveness towards others is implicit in suicides and in suicide attempts – except in rare and exceptional circumstances.

In short, we cannot sacrifice our ego if we are not aware of our own shadow, i.e. of all the facets (from drives to relational or ideative facets) that we do not freely accept as constitutive parts of our personality. This rule holds for the collectivity too, taken as a "corporative personality."[32]

Given that human life is collective, interdependent, and given that the community is the product of an ability to "imagine alternatives," in as much as it is the cultural elaboration of phylogenetic heredity, the result is that the power of possible visions must be channeled, and something precious must be sacrificed, must be put aside so that the "sacred," as a center and a duration of collective life, may order collective existence. But the sacrificial mechanism that is put into place requires a scapegoat,[33] whose symbolic adequacy, as with any cultural event, is subject to enormous variations.

---

[32] On this theme, see Erich Neumann.

[33] The reference here to René Girard's work on sacrifice and scapegoats is obvious; but equally obvious are both my own different view of sacrifice, and the impossibility, in such a short essay, of adequately doing justice to this difference, which relates to monumental questions of history

The scapegoat easily becomes a means by which the community rids itself of internal conflicts, and prevents them from developing. The scapegoat is ideal for this role given the mechanism of pseudo-speciation, which transforms cultural differences into differences of species, attenuating the natural inhibitions toward intra-specific destruction. In this sense, the move to a radical internalization of sacrifice has not only an individual meaning, but rather encourages us to come to terms with all victimary mechanisms. And in the end it becomes a sort of prophecy concerning the survival of the human species when contending poles engage in reciprocal demonization in an irrevocably global space, like the present, which posits universal interdependence as a structural condition for cohabitation. Thus today coming to terms with our own shadow becomes a historical necessity, and in this perspective, molecular analytic work takes on a specific social importance that concerns cultural destinies.

It is clear that we must think in terms of a cultural program of learning, whose progressive validity for the species can only be measured in millennia, and which in very different forms reconnects with religious attempts at salvation, and the efforts of many philosophies: there is an enormous step from the functionality of pseudo-speciation in conditions that are relatively independent of other cultural formations, to the transformation of pseudo-speciation into individual differentiation, which is necessary to survival in conditions of global interdependence.

Nevertheless, external projection onto a scapegoat is certainly not the only way to avoid necessarily confronting our shadow.

In certain cases, when our ego is strong, failing to recognize our own shadow can, through compensation, lead to being marked by the superego's negative judgement, and therefore by social norms, resulting in an unconscious sacrifice to the *idola fori*, and thence to our disappearance into conformist personality.

---

and culture. All the more so because, as far as I know, Girard himself never discusses Neumann's "psychology of the scapegoat" (cf. *Tiefenpsychologie*) as applied to collective history.

At the other extreme, when the ego is weak, the unconscious shadow invades space and acts out a true dissociation, resolving the sacrifice of the ego into the loss of its essential functions.

Or again, the danger of a shadow overburdened by a lack of recognition accumulates in powerful paranoid defenses that deny the ego an adequate capacity to deal with the world; in this case, the ego refuses every sacrifice, for it does not feel capable, yet it denies its own inadequacy, which results in a negative reaction in the face of all possible acceptance of frustration.

In spiritual paths, the subtlest and most difficult temptation to recognize is often that of being too eager to sacrifice, which however is used as an overblown, hidden exaltation of the ego itself. The sacrifice becomes more or less consciously something to brag about.

It is no coincidence then that the death of Baal-Shem-Tov, the initiator of the Hasidim who considered pride to be the root of all sin, is described in these terms:

> Then he bade them cover him with a sheet. But they still heard him whisper: "My God, Lord of all worlds!" And then the verse of the psalm: "Let not the foot of pride come upon me."[34]

This brief Hasidic tale manages delicately to express what innumerable pages of spirituality incessantly repeat as the center and goal of any initiation to spiritual life: the sacrifice of the ego. These words are in fact meant to be Baal-Shem-Tov's final teaching. And if the master needs to repeat it to himself and to others in his last breath, this means that we must never stop re-beginning from the center, i.e. from sacrifice, internalized and expressed as a "prayer," as the deepest wish, the wish of wishes, the essence of wishing itself. Indeed, does "praying to God" not mean precisely expressing the essence of desire, desire led to its essence by despoiling itself of its inessential aspects, or by moving beyond them, following their impetus? In this sense, sacrifice is the fulfillment of a wish, and the sacrifice of praise is its celebration.

[34] Martin Buber, (1949), p.84.

To use terms more closely related to psychology, we might say that the sacrifice of the ego is authentic only when it is a conscious move toward "individual harmonization."[35] Individual harmonization obviously points to the figure of the whole, but a whole that recognizes lack as an external and internal limit. The whole as relation, as inter-intra-being, is originally constituted as a relation of lack, and therefore of desire for each of its parts, a lack that the wholeness of the whole does not fill, but rather reveals to be infinite.

The tendency toward equilibrium among parts does not mean there is no tension, or that parts can be substituted or superimposed. Moreover, the individual whole is the individuation of a multi-individual whole, and as such distinguishes itself from every other individuation of the same whole. And here being aware of limits prevents us from imagining the possibility of a super-individual whole that has not in its turn been individuated. It is only in this way that the sacrifice of the ego continues to be distinct from a representation of the moment of alienation, and thus of manipulative subjection to a higher power,[36] whether this be a sacred or profane institution.

From this comes a criterion for judging institutions, depending upon whether they pursue functional subjection, or agree not to explain the self-realizing force of the "freedom of vision," in its liberation and the limitation of will. Clearly this "renunciation" is something whose only necessary pre-

---

[35] I use this term in place of "individuation" in order to differentiate what I mean from some aspects of the "process of individuation" as Jung understands it. In particular, "individual harmonization" implies achieving a form of equilibrium among the different components of one's personality taken in their historical, cultural context, and thus also among the components of received and reworked cultural models (myths). Jung however sees in the process an originary, archetypal tendency, at the border between nature and culture, which is characteristic of each historical period, however differently it is incarnated. As I have already said with regard to pre-modern and pre-capitalist eras, I here mean a tendency toward "exemplarity." Moreover, Jung sees individuation as a sort of ulteriority with respect to sharing common traits, one that is freed from all conditions, for it has paid its whole debt. I, on the other hand, see individual harmonization as an obviously singular and unrepeatable deepening of interdependence.

[36] "Any god that ... maintains and reinforces foreignness, hierarchies, divisions, is an idol that must be destroyed. There is only one path to freedom, even if the Liberator's names are multiple." Mario Cuminetti, p. 45.

conditions are the pre-oedipal and oedipal renunciation of the objects of one's drives, and relational objects of attachment. It consists precisely of a veritable "sacrifice," repressing the claims which the "I" has "put aside," and which therefore become "sacred," in order to be able to express the whole desire that orients precisely by persisting in its unattainable lack.[37]

In order to approach the "sacrifice of the 'I'" in psychoanalytic and philosophical terms, we might consider "representation:" passing beyond the letter without literalizing any interpretation of the letter seems to me to be the constant exercise of the sacrifice of the egoic intellect and will. Access to the symbolic dimension implies sacrificing claims to exhaustive representation in every language, as in Magritte's famous painting of a pipe which has the words, "This is not a pipe," written beneath it. It is only in this way that we can be in harmony with the vitality of every language beyond the egoic possession of the meaning of the representation.[38] Even the repetition of former attachment relations, in the pride of analytical or educational transference, points to a representational beyond and an opening toward a symbolism of affect. And this symbolic dimension is quite different from any casual expression or deliberate

---

[37] Some pages of Thomas Merton (1961) are truly amazing, particularly those that discuss the sacrifice of the ego, giving insight into a non-psychoanalytic unconscious that stems from Christian mysticism and Zen illumination. Unfortunately, there are too many to cite, so I will limit myself to the following quotation: "But this void is by no means a mere negation. It would be more helpful for Western minds to call it a pure affirmation of the fullness of positive being, though Buddhists would prefer to stick to their principle, neither affirming nor negating." (p. 27) Or again, in a different tradition, which, in my opinion, transposes the same insight onto the ethical plane: "For it is written: 'He hangeth the world over nothingness,' and the Talmud comments on this: 'The world rests upon him who, in the hour of conflict, reduces himself to nothing, and does not say anything against those who hate him." Martin Buber, (1949), p. 218. On positivity as different from the negation of negation, and hence of all negation, both on the ontological plane as well as on the ethical, political one, see Luigi Vero Tarca, 2001a.

[38] In its character as a continuation of the "sacrifice of representation," sandplay is a useful exercise: it is precisely the fact that it never perfectly corresponds to one's intention, given the quasi-necessity of using the available miniatures, that suggests the move to the symbolic dimension. Even more immediate is the need to "put aside" a voluntary and precise conceptual representation, made nearly impracticable by the type of expressive material available. For a complete presentation of sandplay, see Paolo Aite.

prohibition to think intellectually and willingly. Quite the contrary: what we need is the honesty to labor around the concept until it gives way in the face of its own labor, and decides to gather unthought but felt revelations of sense from the *intuitive synthesis* of the material in question.

This appearance of a meaning that is unplanned and unthought by the ego is the event that corresponds, with a few differences in my opinion, to what Jung called the "Self," the new center of the conscious and unconscious personality, once the "I" has consciously renounced being its center and guide.

Surely we can imagine something similar when we try to bring together phenomena such as conversion or illumination. It is wrong to imagine that conversion and illumination are terms that are appropriate for religious experience, but not for philosophical experience. Quite the contrary, in fact, for in as much as this latter corresponds to a practice, it requires continual conversion, and tends toward illumination, continually provoking a decentering of egoity, as Pierre Hadot's works have amply shown with respect to ancient Hellenistic and Roman philosophy.[39]

As I have already mentioned, the radical internalization of sacrifice takes up a central theme of universal spirituality and, in particular, of the Judeo-Christian spirituality from Isaiah (*Isaiah* 1:11) to the *Miserere* (*Psalms* 51), and all the way to Peter's first epistle (*1 Peter* 2:5): sacrifice becomes spiritual sacrifice. In the apostolic story, the crucified Messiah takes the place of the sacrificial victim – and even that of the ancient cursed of the Law (*Deuteronomy* 21:23) – and thus of every scapegoat; thus every sacrifice is overcome and revealed (*Galatians* 3:13-14; *Hebrews* 7:27 and 10).

No sacrificial projection is more acceptable than that of the Messiah taking the place of the cursed; indeed, the path of spiritual sacrifice seems to be illu-

---

[39] I ought to make clear that from this point of view the difference between an ancient plan for philosophical practice and a contemporary one does not consist so much in the end, but rather in the means: the historical difference of cultures and the different role played by individuals and their social roles in them make a plan for philosophical practice necessary, one which methodologically begins with biography and integrates the biographical trajectory into the universal that it is. But this does not alter the fact that, in their different ways, conversion and sacrifice of the ego, as well as desire and illumination, are the guiding constants of experience.

minated by the path of the kenosis (the emptying of egoic claims) and of compassion: salvation is born of knowing itself to be the suffering that is common to that and to those whom we see as an abomination. In Biblical language, the one who is nailed to the cross is cursed by God; a new and different life, a new and different center of resurrection is conceivable only through this passage, which redeems every malediction by hanging the figure of the Messiah over the gates of Hell.

8 The Cosmopolitical Age and the Ethics of Solidary Self-Realization

With compressed intensity the spirit of the age expresses the energy that runs through the whole social body, and there is no doubt that its first expression is to unify the entire species and planet Earth. The population of men, as some people have proudly called themselves, has become a planetary reality. But this process does not imply flattening and homogenizing everyone into indefinite numbers of identical hordes. Culture's natural tendency to create differences and alternatives has not disappeared, nor is it likely to do so in the next few generations. The danger lies precisely in the juxtaposition of isolated, unconsidered actions: the glocalism that arises is insidiously soaked in destruction, and fails to respect any traditions; at the other extreme, the pseudo-speciative tendency of cultures haphazardly reacts to the threat, fomenting clashes that heighten identitary fantasies.

A double task therefore presents itself imperatively: firstly, we must develop a guiding image and criteria for belonging to the universal we have become, and secondly, we must head towards differentiation in the awareness of biographical construction. Humanity in the cosmopolitical age may find an ideal composition of its essential conflict by joining planetary universality to biographical individuality. This assertion clearly sees in utopia a regulative idea of reason, the asymptotic point that measures the approximations that are unable to reach it; it is a moral value that can be posed only by ethical reflection. Its immediacy is entirely enclosed in things; it is built upon the spiral of economic accumulation that encompasses the whole planet, and raises the problem of whether political representation is to provide an adequate institutional structure, but it is not yet able to solve the problem.

But this value is far from shaping the structure of individuals' judgements and motivations and the slow construction of parallel institutional structures, as would be necessary. The remaining unconscious nexus defends itself through opposition: the division widens; the withdrawal of a superficially eccentric singularization (and one that is easily adapted to the masses) corresponds to the planetary interconnection among things, as does too a psychological abyss into which personal history loses all connection to the common history that it expresses.

The natural tendency towards differentiation, stripped of cultural elaborations worthy of the signs of the times, turns into an ethnocentric protest, which at its worst is racist and fundamentalist, and thus stages a grotesque celebration of a poorly-understood history. As usual, an uncomfortable truth that one wishes to suppress is at work in pathological symptoms: the thing-universalism that forcefully imposes itself, realizes and conceals the forever-repeated original sin of the universalisms that have been imposed and conceived up to now. They have used the universal as a justification for and concealment of totally egotistical interests; they have dishonored and tarnished the images of love and universal freedom, and by so doing have covered up crimes of exclusion, oppression, exploitation, sexism and even genocide. Their apparent communist enemies have been no better: the proletarian international has always ended up whitewashing bloody exploits waged in the name of reasons of state. Western religions and philosophies, including scientific, technological ideologies, have been partially infected. The malign shadow that has been its projection has shrouded every type of universalism in suspicion.

We thus find ourselves in a situation of real universalism precisely when we have lost faith in any possible universalism. This effort to expel universal ideas and values from minds and hearts implicitly colludes with the competition for domination that each objectively reproduces and reinforces when it disqualifies the universal and struggles to impose its particular perspective. The strength of anti-universalist arguments generally comes by measuring universalist claims against a standard of perfect universalism: from ancient philosophy to Hegel and even to the critical traditions (Marxism and Freudianism, among others), one implacably sees how the proclamation of universality and totality has been built on exclusion and on the ethnic, social and sexual negation of those who think differently. And this is where criticism shows us a way out: we needn't renounce every effort, but we must purify and perfect every one of our conceptions and expressions of the universal. And this holds for religions, political and social doctrines, philosophies and depth psychologies.

If every universal religion examined itself critically, it would find, in its highest moments of contemplation and practice, a path to harmony with the other experiences of the divine and of meaning. The idea, or intuition, that they all encompass may perhaps be expressed thus: "There is only one God; God is all the names of the gods and of the world; God has No Name." Every word and every tradition is a path that is interrupted where it meets the divine, and it goes on with the knowledge of its infinite descriptive deficiency.

The same exclusive claim of philosophical truths can reveal a way of differentiating the original freedom of culture, and therefore, of the possibility of meaning: the exclusivity of truth can be rethought as freedom, and become universally inclusive, capable of accepting as different even utterances that deny its existence. Harmony has a relation even to disharmony; disharmony, on the other hand, cannot even establish a relationship with itself. Choosing the good does not mean destroying evil; choosing evil implies its own self-destruction. All of this becomes thinkable and practicable if the universal is joined to individuality, in which it is always present and lives, and if individuality is recognized in its essential, cosmopolitical constitution.

In the age of individualization, the social links that everyone depends upon cannot be represented only, or mainly, as an external or exterior force. A form of domination is thereby reproduced that is stripped of any serious consensus and active participation, and is therefore forced into a permanent instability, into endemic fear and ever higher costs of protection. Stripped of recognition, the complete nexus of interdependence of everyone and everything is visible through competition, struggle, and all-out war: the greatest link must live and make itself felt as its opposite, as uncontrolled a-cosmia. In the age of global economic accumulation, the market is no longer limited to a civilization's economic dimension, but has become the one-dimensional civilization of the economy. No qualitative alternative can open up if it does not break with individuality and with the very form of social linkage.

This is the moment when the contribution of depth psychologies, as they have been taken up and developed by an ethics of solidary self-realization, can become a universal event. What is under scrutiny in this dual realization is the original root of social linkage, the possibility of re-evoking and reliving its history in order to rethink it with greater awareness. And in order for this awareness to be individual, it must attain to the reality that touches it the deepest, i.e. being put unsurpassably into complete relation with other humans and with the biosphere. This is certainly a long, difficult path, distant in its goal, in as much as it is entirely here and now in its effort to leave itself and the circle of its kind. Its utopia, which gathers together all those who live on earth (according to the etymological meaning of "ecumenical"), is the diffusion of an elective family relation that goes beyond social connections of cultural pseudo-speciation in historically denominated hegemonic forms: relations of blood and territory, political obligation and economic gain. This is a long march towards the horizons of history, where discovering the common origin in the communion of the living can lead to an ethical development as conscious, autonomous sharing – i.e. which is universally and individually free – of what we are able to regulate and what we must put up with.

Utopia and the ethics of solidary self-realization deliberately take up the original hopes of many religious paths; indeed they continue their search for the discernment of the spirit and of the times. In their aspiration towards a virtuous and happy community life, myths and ideas, religions and philosophies may be considered projects for the possible behavior for the species, whose apprenticeship takes thousands of years. Or reciprocally, for the way of thinking that we are calling "figural narrative," the desire to return to the continuity of this ideal genealogy may represent myth at work in the deep, hidden intention of centuries of demythification: thousand-year-old paths that reemerge in the "scientific" prospects of learning and changing the world.

⑨ Exercises in Philosophical Practices

How do we practice philosophy as a path to life? The first answer is: the way it was practiced by the ancient philosophical schools. Pierre Hadot's reconstructions form the basis of this first response: he has dedicated numerous rich, wisdom-like works to philosophy as the indissoluble nexus of philosophical discourse and philosophical way of life, as it was practiced specifically through spiritual exercises. This response is necessary, but insufficient. Salvaging and restoring the ancient paths to wisdom, once again taking up the spiritual forces of the great Western tradition is a decisive, gripping task; it is also a renewed source of inspiration, but for its own existence, for its intrinsic quality as the expression and formulation of a lifestyle, it requires a renewal of philosophical practices that responds to our history and interacts with its living spirit.

1. Here I will list only a few of the spiritual exercises from ancient philosophy, for a description of which, Pierre Hadot's works are indispensable: meditating on the vastness of the world with reference to itself; paying attention to the present; imminently simulating the day of one's death; examining one's own behavior; remembering the rules of life prescribed by the philosophical orientation that one has decided to follow; training in dialectical argumentation, but only towards the goal of placing argumentation and refutation under a logos that is recognized as a criterion that stands above the disputants and the object of discussion.

We may generally observe that the common goal of these exercises is to create the habit of going beyond the passions that tie us to our egoity as the center and standard of experience; as such they are important and effective for us as well. Secondly, as always in pre-modern practices, they aim at exemplarity, an ideal model towards which we tend. They do no erase individual difference; rather it becomes a way of realizing an exemplary model.

It is precisely for this reason that I believe that ancient exercises – however useful they are for distancing oneself from and moving beyond the personality's egoic centering (obviously I mean people who already have a strong ego, including teachers with enough psychological competence) – must be developed in the direction of a *biographical philosophy*, of the sort that we propose. And this implies certain differences with regard to the ancient practices. The first difference is that one's philosophical itinerary must be biographically constructed, i.e. it must derive from biographical experience. In addition it must measure itself against that experience by attempting to understand and enhance it along the lines of meaning that one's biography requires and delimits. In the end, there is no itinerary that is valid for everyone who follows one school, and hence for everyone who loves wisdom and dedicates his or her existence in a quest for it. The correct path in this case are all paths that valorize individual difference rather than imitate an exemplary model.

We reach the common goal of ancients and moderns by following the stages of exemplary imitation (for the ancient), and those of individual unrepeatability (for the modern). The ancients achieved individuation through exemplarity; conversely for the moderns, we achieve exemplarity through individuation; nevertheless the goal of both is the same.

The second difference between the ancient exercises and those that we propose in order to complete them is a consequence of the distinction between exemplarity and individuation: though it presents itself as one school among others, the distinctive character of biographical philosophy – which includes historical, biographical psychology for appropriately understanding each person's possible itinerary – is that it uses the methods and techniques of every school indifferently. Its distinctively ecumenical nature consists precisely in this. And this ecumenism is not ashamed of its intentional "syncretism," understood as the possible coexistence and cooperation of different theoretical and practical components, which have been made compatible by the fact that they are directed toward the valorization of individuals' differences.

"Syncretism" is a common agreement about potentially divergent positions towards a common objective, and I include the etymology of the word in this definition. All the same, we could not speak strictly of syncretism with regard to biographical philosophy, if we wished thereby to indicate a position that aimed at all costs to synthesize positions that were originally divergent or autonomous. Here the biographical element predominates, and syncretism has the ecumenical function of recognizing precisely the biographical validity of the different paths that others have taken. In other words, from the point of view of biographical philosophy, one may follow a precise direction, even a precise orthodoxy with its own dogma, without mixing it with anything else. It is in the breadth of recognizing "apparently" divergent paths, as well as in the selective criterion of biography, that the difference obtains between other, usually mutually exclusive, philosophical models and biographical philosophy.

If a horizontal panoramic view reveals the syncretic composition of the paths that we have taken, a close-up would show eclectic compositions, in the case of those who do not have recourse to traditionally well-defined expressions, i.e. it would show that we have used different perspectives that are capable of mutual inclusion.

In fact I would say that the salient features of biographical philosophy are its syncretism, with its communitary dimension, and its eclecticism, with its individual dimension, both capable of containing any orthodoxy that has been stripped of its exclusivity. This syncretism and eclecticism turn however towards ecumenism, as a universal utopia of the global pact of balance and peace, and they are unified by the process and structure of biographical construction.

2. What are the particular modalities of this philosophy, besides the usual ones of teaching, of writing, of dialogue and argumentative debate that aims at disproof, of listening and studying in order to learn the foundations and history of the discipline? Given that we do not intend to replace the philosophical disciplines as they are already taught in schools and universities, but only to complete them, and thereby partially free ourselves of them, I will list a few possible exercises of biographical philosophy that I have met with or created in the course of more than twenty-five years of personal practice: psychoanalytic,

autobiographical practice, meditation and the practice of communicative experimentation and didactic philosophy.

The ideas we present here are part of an effort to renew philosophy, in as much as philosophy may be or may appear to be scattered and arbitrary. Given its origins and modalities of exercise, our effort is similar to but independent of the experiments in "practical philosophy" that have been conducted in the last twenty years in Germany, and have thence spread to Europe and the United States. Obviously, in accordance with its spirit, my proposal does not intend unilaterally to define the domain of philosophical practices, and it is therefore open to comparison and collaboration. This does not in any way imply smoothing over differences in formulation and styles of conduct in the name of institutional, associative constructions or of recognition by any particular profession. I mean rather an unfettered search for meaning that is directed at people's existential questions and conducted by reconsidering the richness of the philosophical tradition and inventing new forms: and this could be the limit of the terrain common to different philosophical practices, their meeting place, and the site of their divergence.

As far as I am concerned, a mutually exclusive debate, along the lines of a diatribe, that aims to impose some presumed truth is precisely one of the old modalities of philosophical debate that must be abandoned. Associative, professional forms of renewed philosophical practice are even more clearly secondary problems, which one must nevertheless keep separate from the pseudophilosophical invitation that conceives of the human as a necessary request for meaning, and calls "philosophy" the self-awareness and practice of that necessary questioning. And here this need is understood as inscribed in the conditions of biological life itself, once the human distinguishes itself according to its cerebral capacity to reproduce, and to some degree control and transform, its own imagine of its surroundings and of itself.

3. Obviously in the first place, practicing biographical philosophy means "marking life's path," a mark on *bios*. Thus life reaches its reflexive state, searching for a possible design that is born first of all from the attentive recognition of events, well beyond the direction of our immediate needs, desires and

intentions. Our exposition already opens the possibility and prepares the way for recognizing unconscious tendencies that are potently active in us. Misunderstanding these tendencies is a source of added suffering, it precludes a larger integration, and it is the symptom of egoic over-investment, which is forgetful of the essential co-belonging, the inter-intra-being of the Self within the human community (which produced it, and now supports and surrounds it) and within the life of the planet.

The techniques available for creating an autobiographical and biographical disposition for oneself are numerous. I might mention keeping a diary (which may or may not be organized, but which at least contains a record of daily happenings, memory, fantastic and oneiric elements, planning, meditation and rational argumentation), autobiographical writing, and recounting significant moments of one's life to others. Although this is not the place for further clarification of these techniques, it is worthwhile to note a few things.

As far as diaries are concerned, I would like to point out that intentionally bringing together different dimensions of experience and variations in time, which have been recorded and cannot for the moment be corrected, allows us to observe ways of organizing experience, and therefore structures of meaning that organize themselves independently of our rational awareness of the present and the will of the moment. If we write each entry by avoiding connections to preceding entries, then reading the diary reveals unintentional macro-connections, autonomous unravellings of meaning, which for this very reason invite us to integrate and correct, putting us into contact with an intelligence that is wider and more acute than life. Regularity in this task helps to relativize the ego's importance, to come closer to a feeling of impermanence in time, and to experience a more spiritual dimension. And by "spiritual" I mean precisely the appearance of a meaning that consciousness has not yet been able to formulate by itself, and a meaning that is indeed often in singular contrast with its assumptions and preferences.

Keeping a diary is a fundamental exercise in the practice of biographical philosophy because it allows the day and night-time records of thought to interact; it acts upon temporal compartmentalization, making them objective, and invites us to review our memory; it is based on expectation, freed from routine, and at the same time it allows us to wait for revelation; in real time it compares news events with one's plans, actions and calculations; it contaminates considered arguments with figural accounts, and vice-versa. Altogether these features turn the diary into a record within the organism of one's biographical metabolism, almost an alter ego, intimate confidant and the most complete, privileged witness of one's immediate consciousness. A diary is therefore the principal path to *over-awareness*, which biographical philosophy aims at.

On the other hand, keeping a diary on biographical-philosophical lines also has an immediate value, beyond its structure. The pages of Marcus Aurelius that Pierre Hadot has examined offer a good example of the sort of meaning that the exercise of writing for oneself can take on in philosophical auto-didacticism. One must keep in mind however that the biographical philosopher does not apply the dogmas of a particular school, but rather finds, renews and constructs his or her own dogmas as reflection, meditation and intuition about his or her life experience gradually permit.

Hadot writes:

> Such writing exercises thus lead necessarily to incessant repetitions, and this is what radically differentiates the *Meditations* from every other work. Dogmas are not mathematical rules, learned once and for all and then mechanically applied. Rather, they must somehow become achievements of awareness, intuitions, emotions, and moral experiences which have the intensity of a mystical experience or a vision. This spiritual and affective spirituality is, however, quick to dissipate. In order to reawaken it, it is not enough to reread what has already been written. Written pages are already dead, and the *Meditations* were not made to be reread. What counts is the reformulation: the act of writing or talking to oneself, right now, in the very moment when one needs to write. It is also the act of composing with the greatest care possible: to search for that version which, at a given moment, will produce the greatest effect, in the moment before it fades away, almost instantaneously, almost as soon as it is written. Characters traced onto some medium do not fix anything: everything is in the act of writing.[40]

[40] Pierre Hadot, 1998, p. 51.

And again, to reinforce the nexus between repeating an exercise and the essence of philosophical life:

> This was an exercise of writing day by day, ever-renewed, always taken up again and always needing to be taken up again, since the true philosopher is he who is conscious of not yet having attained wisdom.[41]

As for telling life stories, or fragments of autobiography, in my experience it is important to have a set of communicative rules that foster a calm opening and the certainty of being welcomed. [For these rules see the preceding section on biographical-solidary communication.] In any case, I will say that life stories can achieve the goal of reintegrating the subjectivity of living experience in communicative experience, despite its being difficult to share; moreover it does so in such a way that the individual feels that his or her singularity is worthy of an audience, and is authorized to take its place in the world, independently of identifying itself with the opinions and judgements of others.

4. The most important biographical investigation relives one's personal history in emotional, affective and rational comparison with the other. Remembering and reliving necessarily accompany every possible reconstruction, and only reconstruction, with its new perspectives and new feelings, enables us to confront the obstacles that hinder us from confronting both the tasks and problems of the present and our desires and future plans. This is the objective of psychoanalytic and most psycho-therapeutic techniques. It is imperative to integrate them into the practice of biographical philosophy.

This does not mean however that those who intend to dedicate themselves to this group of philosophical practices are obliged to follow all possible formative paths, nor that all philosophers are obliged to have training as analysts: different practices serve as high-water marks against which each person finds his or her own path. Nevertheless, when biographical philosophy is employed in an analytic context (by patients as much as analysts) it certainly encounters a

---

[41] *Ibid.*

very fertile field in terms of the vastness and deepness of transformation and knowledge.

I have already mentioned a few reasons to cultivate these connections; now I would like to point to a feature of relational analysis where the biographer is not only an analyst but, more specifically, a third element which is both a condition and result of the relation. And by relational analysis I mean analysis of the networks of relations that subtend individual experience and that encourage the transformation of autobiographical willingness into "biographical analysis."

In the experimental condition of the relationship with a privileged, competent witness, it is precisely the care for those networks of relations that, in the heat of emotion, attests to emotions, images and thoughts, the primary conditioners of our experience. But it is also in this relation that we participate in the birth of a "meaning" that is not attributable to the pair at work, but to something that, like an autonomous third element, is born from the preparation that is fostered by listening to symbolic figures.

5. In order to go beyond the unilateralness of thought in the common, immediately understandable sense, and the unilateralness of logical argumentation, we must dedicate particular attention to imaginative activity. Attention to the oneiric dimension is already part of our practice, but it is possible to employ other representational capacities that the philosophical, and even psychoanalytic, traditions have neglected in adults, preferring to consign them to supposed infantile expressive registers that they define as primordial, or primitive, or even psycho-pathological. Perhaps this is still a symptom of an imbalance that often atrophies our education in the matter of intuition and representation of our feelings and emotions, thus preparing the terrain for explosions and hypertrophic fashions.

At the same time, appealing to the hand-eye-brain circuit, which, along with upright stature and prehensile hands, is original to human intelligence, is a method that reinvests the integrated whole of human possibilities for meaningful revelation. Here I am thinking not only of active imagination and drawing, but primarily of "sandplay" (or "world play"), which, when it is employed in an analytical context,[42] allows us to express unconscious experiential levels and perspectives of possible meaning that were invisible at the time. The game accomplishes this synthesis of hands and eyes by having the player manipulate miniatures of human and natural situations. Naturally, these considerations are intimately linked to a person's upbringing, and therefore only exemplify a vaster spectrum of possibilities, bioenergetics, psycho-drama, art-therapy, etc.

6. A thorough, constant comparison with one's life story can in many cases lead to retracing certain fundamental reasons whose connections seem to unfold out of range of our conscious consideration and decisions. For this reason we may speak of a myth within biography, of mythobiography. The double movement of "concentric amplification" and circumstantiality facilitates this recognition. In its singularity and transience, concentric amplification brings biographical experience back to generally valid cultural motifs, or even to cultures of other contexts. Thus the conviction that we are closed in the incommunicability of our private life dissipates, and we recognize ourselves in behavior that is expressed in images and stories which obviously take their universality and thousand-year-old constancy from their hereditary phylogenetic roots.

The countermovement of equilibrium is directed toward returning to biographical circumstances in order to identify their differences. Biography refers to the myth that lives it in order to understand itself; myth returns to biography, for it cannot live otherwise; it develops in the contingencies of reality and experiences its potential developments. Yes, myth performs biographical experiments, and this is the dynamism of cultural variation and natural selection. Becoming aware of this is thus a daring, delicate task, for conscious direction can, to some extent, influence that same cultural, i.e. natural, selection with its own interests.[43] What is at stake is indeed the type of human that can emerge from mythobiographical dynamics.

7. Studying and teaching take on a different hue when they are immersed in biographical practices: one's motivation will certainly be more lively, and the

---

[42] See Paolo Aite.
[43] See Eibl-Eibesfeldt, pp. 9-15, where he discusses this thesis, and the related theses of Mayr and Popper.

terrain where different perspectives meet will be more solid and familiar. In the biographical context, study and teaching find a universal standard of comparison that is also proper to each. That standard can direct a program of study, and one's research may make use of all necessary specialization, yet we will understand and fully feel the interconnection only in the very singular specialization of our own life story. The very figure of the teacher changes, and the quality of intersubjective relations takes on great importance beside the traditional transmission of the state of knowledge. It moreover indicates possible lines of research and involves other competent people.

8. How do we exchange life experiences and, both implicitly and explicitly, the perspectives of knowledge incorporated in them or accompanying them, in a mutually positive way? Every affirmation, if it is not connected to personal life, easily becomes a topic of discussion from an external, Archimedean point of view: i.e. the point of view of "God's neutrality" or of impersonal truth. This is one way to limit the damage, or at least the damage slides below our attention and below communicability: whoever feels defeated in the contest suffers abstractly from not being recognized to such an extent that he is unable to articulate it adequately to himself, unless he suspects himself of being overly sensitive.

If, at the other extreme, even a small peephole for communicating oneself opens, it at first seems that there is not enough space for another way of seeing, that any different experience and vision must be disabled. We ought to be clear, however, that personalized controversy is a modern hybrid, in as much as it has shed precisely its character as exercise, losing its function of accustoming us to submitting to a logos that is greater than both participants. This function can be salvaged by assigning the tasks of defending and attacking a thesis to participants independently of their own convictions; thus from the beginning one avoids any type of identification between those who are practicing the dialectic and the ideas that they must support or criticize.

As for the full, philosophical consideration of one's own life experience, a group emerging from this project has experimented with several rules of solidary, biographical communication that are also useful for transmitting knowledge.

i. Even the remotest form of cognition carries with it a link to its own life story; therefore reference to personal experience may accompany all communications.[44]

ii. If one takes into account biographical considerations, then any perspective can be heard within the conditions of its origin, and it follows that we can accept different perspectives and conceptions, and not only in a methodological or purely formalistic sense. Communication is not a rare commodity that is likely to disappear through use. On the contrary, use enlarges and deepens communication, and so at least some of the reasons for the struggle to attain a dominant position disappear. In communication, once the argument about the commodity's scarcity has been stripped away, the struggle for dominance reveals that it is merely a struggle for power.

iii. Just as the discussion concerning exclusive characteristics of a certain affirmation can be overcome by a warm reception, even substitutive interpretation (which is generally summarized by saying that "that which appears is a mask for something that is acting secretly") can be abandoned by the listener who then enters into dialogue: when even substitutive interpretation truly reveals what was hidden, it only leads to the speaker forming further, more or less justified, tormented defensive arguments. I do not however wish to deny the validity of interpreting defensive arguments, but any interpretation must be rigorously circumscribed within the psychoanalytic context, with all of its caveats, and always with the express consent of whoever wishes to follow that path.

iv. Every different way of seeing things, on the part of those who are listening and participating, can be offered as a variation on a point of view (as an anamorphic offering) that is connected to the different formative, biographical circumstances that have conditioned it and promote it. An offer that may either be declined or internalized can also be used to reconsider

---

[44] I believe that it is theoretically possible in an "advanced" group to leave this reference implicit, as far as is necessary at the beginning, to train together in explicit biographical terms. Nevertheless, until now, I have no experience that might confirm the plausibility of this communicative experiment.

what one has experienced and what has found a provisional form of expression. This way of giving back to the other has the advantage of opening one's own world to possible experiences of different worlds, and it can even help to diminish the sense of loneliness that often goes with the particularity of one's "destiny," if it is experienced as a painful form of exclusion. The anamorphosis of destiny could even offer the possibility of perceiving never-before imagined alternatives.

v. Aggressiveness should not be demonized. It must nevertheless be rigorously thought through and internalized, as one silently searches for its reasons and examines its forms. (I mean strictly with respect to these few techniques, and have no intention of extending the practice to one's whole daily life, public or private, nor to all possible philosophical exercises, as is clear in the case of a dialectical argument.) We therefore advise a sort of self-analysis with respect to aggression, even constructive aggression, without however externalizing it.

Ideally one can practice biographical, solidary communication by connecting it to different ends, beyond the rules that we are listing here.

1. Practicing biographico-solidary communication aims at being a way of "communicating oneself," and therefore a way of forming a stronger, more intimate connection between interiority and its original function, which is to put us into relation with others. It is a symbol of a family connection that is no longer conferred by descendancy, randomness or destiny, but that is free in its choice of elective affinities. And it is also a sign of a finality that moves beyond a group of friends and aims at universality.

2. The solidarity of self-realization is the most proper dimension of self-realization itself: by this I mean that self-realization occurs in the solidary link that is the origin and destiny of the self. There is really no need to list the possible ways of dedicating oneself to others: these vary depending upon traditions and levels, and offer each person a possible path. The biographical practice of communication does not replace works with words.

Rather, it attempts to find a psychic and spiritual way for different solidary practices, where opening one's heart – as far as is possible – is joined with sharing gestures and objects.

3. The realization of the self in solidarity is a utopian idea, a teleological image, an idea of reason which we use to measure the distance between our lives and world and an ideal of justice that is founded on the unfolding of individual potential. And this path obviously leads away from the constructive principle of our civilization of economic accumulation, in its triumphant version of global capitalism, as well as in the vanquished version of bureaucratic collectivism. Moreover, we can confidently state that our civilization is condemning itself: we can judge it simply by taking seriously the ideas that it proclaims and the promises that it has been making for more than two hundred years. How could it have lasted one minute, especially in the last fifty years, if it truly had to judge itself based on the Universal Declaration of Human Rights, which has been accepted by nations and peoples as a timely, universal table of values? It would be like realizing that one's hair was on fire, as a Buddhist saying has it, though relating to a totally different situation: our civilization would not be able to continue for one second; our clear priority would be to put out the fire.

4. Basing ourselves in biography allows us to make use of and connect different capacities for experience and study, without erasing their differences. Communication and plasticity are the keys, not the abstract abolition of social and technical divisions of capacities and work. It is important to cultivate the nexus among daily life, expressive forms and reflection in a permanent educational search that aims in this direction.

5. It is possible to experience both the roles of guide and master, of disciple and student; they are in fact experienced dynamically and alternately. The goal of philosophical practice in our age must be to avoid getting stuck in one role, while maintaining its traditional richness; today, the complexity of knowledge and the speed of transformation oblige us to search for more flexible methods of transmitting knowledge. But the point of the exercise is

even more profound and implies rethinking egoic claims: it aims to foster the perception of the sense of interdependence and a feeling of humility.

6. The forms of meditation and contemplation that come from different Western and Eastern religious traditions are extremely rich. The Judeo-Christian-Islamic traditions have developed infinite variations on these practices, which one must sift through, paying close attention to individual history and attitudes, in order to find the inspiration for the path that is best adapted to oneself.

As a general criterion we might mention the hesicastic program of cultivating silence, solitude, tranquility and inner rest. For those who are familiar with depth psychologies, we might mention the meditative practice called "active imagination," in which one enters into dialogue with spontaneous images. Conversely, I believe that many of the Vietnamese Zen master Thich Nhat Hahn's meditative exercises are particularly adapted, psychologically speaking, for listening and for transforming emotions.

As I have already said, the appropriateness of these suggestions depends upon one's nature and personal history. What matters is to come closer to the mystery that contains and constitutes us. Re-visiting different meditative traditions and prayers is really only one way, one method to find those forms of wisdom that can perceive the signs of the times. Or in other words, a method that is applicable at a time when we are obliged to cohabit with and are often contaminated by different philosophical schools and religious doctrines. Our goal remains the same throughout time: recognizing the paths that lead us to contemplate the communion of everything with everyone, and our co-belonging to the mystery that lies beyond (before, after and within) every gesture and every word.

7. In the process of renewal – and in order precisely to achieve renewal – we must pay particular attention to tradition. What remains of the philosophical exercise is tied to "knowing how to read" and "knowing how to argue and disprove," and thus to the fields of hermeneutics, logic and the dialectic. These philosophical practices, which have been honed by the careful study

of the last few centuries, are still so rich that they obviate the need for any list or description of them.

And yet I just mentioned that when the dialectical art of argumentation and disproof is brought back to its original purpose of identifying a reason that rises above a particular debate, it can regain its enormous educational value precisely if it is employed strictly as an exercise, in which the participants have no particular attachment to the positions they must defend or attack.

In our spiritual tradition, and beyond the indications of modern hermeneutics and the rediscovery of different styles of philosophical interpretation, even "reading" texts can make use of the ancient methods of *lectio divina*, as applied to any text. Actually, paying attention to lexical and spiritual constructions, literary genres and rhetorical figures is a part of any serious reading. But one might also add the *meditatio* – i.e. a questioning of the text that implicates one's personal experience and understanding – as well as the *contemplatio* and *oratio*, the act of concentrating for a moment on whomever or whatever speaks to us through the words that we are considering: if a monk or a Christian reader naturally thinks about his or her God, every other reader may contemplate the breath of a spirit in any text when that spirit has moved the events of a humanity that belongs to its own being in the world.

8. The relationship to one's own body in movement and to animal and vegetable life is an enormous domain for exercise that is well known to ancient philosophy and a source of infinite considerations for the moderns. "Nature" can, and to some extent must, be the theater of philosophical practice, both as a game or work, and as contemplation, research, curiosity and physical exercise. Our world is discouraged in part because it is no longer accustomed to the rhythm of the living, to its immediate presence.

A feeling of limits and a feeling of immensity, relativizing the ego and accepting interdependence, the need for defense and compassion, disorientation and order of meaning in a map of one's journey, consistency of means, the control and presence of the end in the movements of a body at work, the interrelation among stages of the body and emotions of the soul, metaphors of "birth, procreation and death," all of these things, and many others, can be brought to the fore by paying close attention to the philosophical exercise that is inherent in a dynamic perception of the body and in the life of nature.

9. Practice needs a place and time, indeed different places and different times that express, if only symbolically, individual and communitary dimensions, affinities and distances. It is especially necessary to demarcate a space-time unit that is free of other occupations, or better, in which any other occupation takes place in an atmosphere that is pervaded by and attentive to philosophical exercise. Its unfolding can be broad and precise, pervading daily life without becoming invasive or obsessive.

We must include community practice alongside the idiorhythmic nucleus of practices that have been selected and modelled on an individual trajectory. First of all because individuality and its history are built of collective material, to such an extent that the process of individuation (or of individual harmonization, as I have re-baptized it within the domain of biographical philosophy) can be thought of as the emergence of investigation into awareness, sympathy and compassion, the essential interdependence of everyone with everyone and everything. The places and rhythms of individual practices must be left on the idiorhythmic side of this proposal of rules for philosophical life. Community spirit can be developed in periodical *philosophical practice retreats*, built around practicing philosophical discourse and exercises, and conducted according to the rules of biographical, solidary communication.

Obviously the choice of place – especially one that changes from year to year – is as important as the rule that fosters an atmosphere of attentive, free, welcoming and open hearing, for it also expresses the ecumenical spirit of biographical philosophy, without excluding preferences or a relative identification with a particular place, and is perhaps thus more adapted to the mobility of our age. Thought of as a house that welcomes and gathers, every station of the itinerary becomes an occasion for integration and differentiation, for a richness that belongs to different traditions and that is available to the individual and the group. The place transmits living practice, which today is almost certainly always religious, but which thereby pre-serves an enormous philosophical inheritance. In as much as it is a circle that contains spiritualities of different traditions, *lay spirituality* (which is lay due to the agreement of different belongings in a mutual recognition of values) offers a reason for communication and community. Moreover, lay spirituality is able to take on the contributions of both faiths and traditional religiousness and more recent forms and a-religious spirituality, on the common terrain of a group of shared philosophical practices.

10 A Few Thoughts on Freedom, Truth and Individuality

Does the philosophical claim to truth not already invalidate itself? Everyone pulls it towards himself, putting his best arguments on display in disproving his adversaries'. It even seems as though doing philosophy consists in "overcom-ing" every preceding truth, as if by disproving all those before us, we could legitimize a new attempt, or, conversely, that we should adhere to a school or line of thinking, developing some hitherto neglected aspect. Today, doing phi-losophy implies doing the history of philosophy, but no longer with the pathos of Hegelian or historical truth, as if it were understood that philosophy belongs to the past, however decisive and fascinating that past may be: philosophy becomes a philology of culture.

All of this has produced a powerful, erudite arsenal of logical and historical arguments. In the best case scenario, the enormity of historical erudition, com-bined with the nearly perfect state of argumentation, that is bereft of a recog-nizable meaning other than a taste for technical refinement for its own sake, leads to philosophy as the clear, precise laboratory of demonstrations and counterdemonstrations, a general methodology of techniques. In the spirit of formalization characteristic of the age, the seriousness of the ancient search for truth would in some way be confirmed, once the unrealistic ambition to point to some reality and some method of knowing the real as "truth" has been overcome.

Obviously reactions to this line of thought have been considerable, but they either attempted to "overcome" philosophy by transforming the world practically, with the unhappy result that they fell prey to the need for legitimacy on the part of the powers that operate in the name of this same transformation, or they became a very successful rhetorical exercise in evoking the nearly ineffable depths of thought and being, as in Heidegger's case. And this exercise paradoxically ends up reducing every type of philosophizing into philosophical discourse, in precisely the sense that it excludes every biographical trace (and logically any biographical *method*) as irrelevant,[45] while the world itself goes back to explaining the power of the thoughts that describe and guide it. It is therefore not surprising that "shepherds of being" often end up associating themselves to profound-sounding blather.

The word "truth" has thus undergone a double devaluation, for on the one hand it circulates less freely, and on the other it is over-produced.

On the other hand, when we imply that every proclamation of truth intrinsically helps to limit the freedom of whoever thinks differently, we openly ask for the consensus of our age. Has this unhappy drama not been played out and repeated in innumerable circumstances? In the end, freedom that has become truth has been obliged to shed every truth that is different from the rhetoric of continual search and from the mandatory respect of every relative truth.

---

[45] Nevertheless, if cohabitation with biographical philosophy's perspective is quite unlikely, from the Heideggerian point of view, the reverse is very possible: i.e. it is possible that a method of biographical philosophy would express itself in such a way as to acknowledge the results of Heideggerian philosophy as its inspiration and contents. In the latter case, the selective biographical criterion actually allows us to take up any other contribution as its own building material. This occurs with every new cultural formulation, which in general justifies itself as a new way to give form to mutually incompatible cultural inheritances, for it is precisely the new point of view that makes them compatible. Moreover, it seems widely accepted that biographical philosophy can be seen as a new version of eclecticism: I would say that it is in principle eclectic with regard to the composite choice of its contents, even if it can in fact choose not to exercise its eclectic possibility but rather to remain in a well-defined orthodoxy. It is syncretic if taken as a whole, i.e. as the whole of the different contents of different ways of practicing biographical philosophy. And it is ecumenical if one considers its possibility and its intention of universal openness to all cultures and individuals.

As it is nevertheless impossible to allow every presumed attempt against freedom to pass without a reaction, the enemies of relativist schooling have been relegated to the status of fundamentalists, when they have not been outright suspected of terrorism. And often, alas, for many good reasons. But freedom has inevitably set off a chain-reaction in which every type of conflict adds a contrasting twist, and freedom ends up occupying the place of pure negation. And this role is now so deeply established that it brings together competing philosophies.

If one looks at its content, one sees that philosophy – particularly hermeneutics – is busy critiquing every more or less unconsciously metaphysical presupposition of modern science and technology.

If one looks at its methodology, one learns to appreciate the refinement with which the inheritors of analytic philosophy dedicate themselves to the anatomical pathology of argumentation.

In the 150 years since it cut its teeth trying to critique and transform the world, philosophy seems to have consoled itself with the self-legitimizing observation that if the world cannot transform itself, it is at least less adept at critical thinking than philosophy itself. One can therefore settle into the postmodern position that mistrusts any form of knowledge or construction which tempts us to found an idea, thus into the position of those who represent the freedom to which everyone refers. "Perfect critique" becomes the equivalent of "perfect integration." The figure of modern ideology indeed seems to take up where the postmodern fades into the ultra-modern: i.e. the continual, eternal creative destruction, the immovable institution of perennial change, the spirit of the modern that becomes stronger after overcoming every postmodern hurdle. But the opposition or identification of truth and freedom are only two possible ways of relating these two indispensable values.

Can freedom be conceived and practiced as the originary dimension of truth? Can truth be conceived and practiced as the self-reflexive expression, and therefore the self-establishing moment, of the originary dimension of freedom?

If truth – which is single – did not also stretch into the infinitude of freedom, it would remain outside what opposes it. And thus the truth becomes a half-truth; the truth of what is false sunders it and contradicts it as one. If what is false only remains negated or disproved, then with its naked existence it proclaims it partiality, and thence the falseness of the truth that opposes it.

If, on the other hand, the false is gathered into the unity of the true and the false, then the truth exposes the limit that gives falsity its truth. Only then do we understand acutely. Acute understanding is a true understanding of the understanding that transcends the negation of the false by the true. True and false are in fact interchangeable depending upon the perspective and context of their affirmation, but such that for every false proposition there is always a possible world for which it is true. And vice-versa.

In other words, the true-false binary is the transcendental condition of our judgements that employs freedom as the necessary postulate of that same true-false binary. The limit of freedom is the greatest distance between the human species and the guidance of phylogenetic heredity – which is what makes "animals almost always know what to do," and prevents them from building sign systems that can refer to different dimensions of reality, and that can give rise to "false connections" – and at the same time, it is the origin of truth as a problem. This means that true and false are expressions of freedom by which freedom recognizes itself as such, and thus as the truth of freedom. In a positive way, this can teach us the modern truth of freedom.

Truth is thus seen as the dynamic, transcendental dimension of affirmation: since every negation, by its nature as negation, must simultaneously be a negative affirmation, then eschatological, transcendental affirmation (the logical point of meaning, which can be represented in the form of an asymptote, exactly as the figure of the sage stands in relation to the exercise of philosophical life) contains every negation without thereby negating it, indeed, by affirming it as a negation that, as such, affirms itself. Thus affirmation is intrinsic to every negation and to every affirmation, i.e. it is transcendental. And since this act of affirmation contains every possible negation, it is also the logical correlative of the eschatological symbol[46] of an all-inclusive act of affirmation, and of its infinite possible meaning.

Thus negation becomes an instrument for differentiation, taking up different forms of opposition (between opposites, or complements, of privation) as expressions of a unity that is still susceptible to further expression, all the way to the opposition between contradictions in its most extensive form between being and non-being, in which the differentiation that is inherent in every possible discourse operates.

The logos that affirms itself even when it negates its own being – in as much as non-being has expression – exposes the dynamic of differentiating expression that is intrinsic to the nature of transcendental affirmation. Even the absolute negation that nothingness is, or that everything is nothing, expresses, as part of transcendental affirmation, the apophatic difference of an intuition regarding totality, its use of language in order to mark its unsurpassable limit. Which is, moreover, what every mystical experience has always taught.

The fact that being and non-being, and therefore every possible contradiction, belong to transcendental affirmation shows the need for difference to be separate from discourse, and, thus, the need for meaning, which is the relationship among differences. It also shows the need for truth-based discourse, in as much as this must see itself as dynamic, and as an eschatological recall to the all-inclusiveness of all possible paths to truth. The originary freedom of culture unfolds in these infinite paths, reflecting itself in the propriety of every discourse.

All the same it is worthwhile to explain that the freedom that I am writing about is much deeper than any political form of freedom. Deeper because it is its root, but it is also the root of every negation of political and civil liberties. I mean freedom as the biological, or better, the neuro-ethological, capacity to "imagine differently," i.e. to reproduce, and in part control and modify (and therefore to reflect and choose) any representation, in virtue of the combined play between cerebral modules and function; these latter being produced by the

---

[46] In mythobiographical terms: considering the cosmic, theological value of his wounds, this eschatological symbol of all-inclusive affirmation is, in my view, figured in the body of the resurrected Christ.

presence of the neo-cortex and the differentiation of the hemispheres, which in turn are connected to upright stature, panoramic vision, verbal language, and the freeing of the hand for the development of technology.[47]

Thus human nature doubles itself and to some degree makes its phylogenetic inheritance plastically variable. For this reason human kind ceases to have an environment to which it responds according to stable patterns that have already been adapted by natural selection; rather it responds more and more to a world transformed by culture, according to actions that can be established in institutions or that are not destined to last. All the same, even what has been instituted is chosen in the uncertainty of changes in a historically determined environment, into which it places itself and which it quite unpredictably co-determines.

In this space, we propose a modified version of Socrates' assertion that enquiry is the greatest dignity of human life. Once an instinctual hierarchy and the representation of an instinctual road network appear as a form of behavior,[48] transformed and re-used by cultural constructs, it becomes clear that the question of "good" and "evil" becomes both necessary in its position and relatively arbitrary with respect to possible answers. Before it is a dignity to pursue, enquiry is a necessity that must be followed in order for us to survive. And here I mean too that the self-destructive choice of possibilities of survival must pass through a previous enquiry into what constitutes a "good" choice. Again: this means that before arriving at an answer with regard to content – i.e., "what is the good" – we must admit that the good is above all asking ourselves what good it is, because the life that is the source of the question, and of any further good, depends upon it. Therefore the condition for every good is that it allows us to enquire into what good it might be.

---

[47] These factors in the process of homination must be considered in their dynamic, reciprocal interrelation: none of them taken singly can account for the genesis of man's cultural capacities as capacities upon which the survival of the species depends. This is true even in the sense that they could erase its phylogenetic inheritance, which would lead to the species self-destructing.
[48] Eibl-Eibesfeldt, pp. 56-57.

It follows that, as a first good practice, the need for the question leads us to individuate that which fosters this enquiry into the good: thereby philosophical life represents the good, whose search is the condition for every other good.

But when one is faced with the need to guarantee the continuity of different cultures, essential freedom in fact becomes too dangerous a freedom to be witnessed, as Socrates' trial reminds us. It then transpires that the need for the stability of a single, momentary cultural configuration collides with the renewal of the conditions of possibility of any culture. The interests of a cultural configuration imperil the manifestation of the possibility to continue to create alternatives. Precisely for this reason the truth of freedom has often been muzzled by a truth that has repressed its origins, and that does not attempt to immobilize the inevitable transcendental horizon of truth that includes the various reasons for the differentiation between true and false, but attempts rather to stick certain contents onto truth, and to consign "the false and lying gods" to nothingness.

And who were "the false and lying gods"? Fortunately, many of us privileged, ruling Westerners have developed a vast awareness of guilt, one which is entirely justified and which it would be criminal to shed. This makes us cautious and clever: we know that we have slaughtered peoples, animals, forests, seas in the name of Christian and Greco-Roman truth, or of communist, capitalist or civilian progress. In a form of reverse creation we have confirmed the dominion of death, protected by the good conscience of a better life. Finally we know that our gods certainly were false and lying; concerning those of others we can have similarly reasonable doubts. And yet, this bloody unleashing of modern relativism contains a new sacred tension of truth.

Why cannot truth welcome rather than exclude? Why can it not be so welcoming as to welcome even exclusion, without violating its nature as exclusion, leaving to exclusion the will to exclude itself? Why must the contextuality of every cultural construct of values be attributed by right to the impossibility of truth? Why cannot the partiality of every truth, taken as such, constitute the true part of the whole truth, even if what surrounds it inevitably escapes us? This cannot happen as long as we think that truth excludes and disproves nontruth. But truth, experiencing itself in this disproof and negation, experiencing itself as domination and oppression, has negated itself and become non-truth itself, in our eyes and in those of the truth that affirmed itself. For the first time, the universal negation of truth puts us in the position of thinking of truth as in-clusive, capable of seeing all of the non-truths as such only in mutual exclu-sion. Omni-lateral interdependence is their truth; conciliation is the possibility of the truth that assumes as its postulate and pre-condition the interdependence and contextuality of every truth, which is truth in as much as it is the product of freedom.

Meanwhile, the negative feature of modern truth can turn into the positive affirmation of the value that conditions every other value, forever renewing the possibility of continuing to create alternatives: and we might call this an ethics of "cultural survival." We may proceed from this to imagining a regulative ideal: given the possibility of posing alternatives, we can imagine a condition that effectuates an infinite enquiry and goes beyond into the communication of infinite, co-existing possibilities.

The infinitude of questioning goes beyond into the infinity of possible, co-existing answers. The infinite exception of biographies is thus freed in the insti-tution of the conditions of the species' life. In its vocation, philosophy thus serves the individual's freedom, but the constitution of a non-contradictory field is a question of ethical choice: in this sense, which we can attribute to the need for possible alternatives, the possibility of contradiction is necessary to cultural imagination. But in its form as man's cultural nature, this linguistic reference to life puts the value of the oscillation of meanings in the service of renewing alternative potentials. It hopes thereby to include the opposition of contradictory statements in the conciliation of opposites, complements and deprivations, without trying to eliminate that which wishes to remain in the extreme position of negation (the negation that by its internal logic is given to negating even itself).

Therefore if the capacity to imagine differently is the natural, transcendental condition for the freedom that constitutes culture, and if ethics necessarily de-rives from this capacity – given that it is the result of this freedom – it follows that the good implies first of all keeping alternatives open, i.e. perptuating life itself, which is *by nature* cultural life. Secondly, given these original conditions, the good turns out to be insaturable. Its concept is dynamic, transferable and open to ever different and further understandings: one can always imagine a wider, more comprehensive alternative, a new proposal that is able to reconcile the unreconciled, to include the excluded, even if it is always ready to accept that the excluded has excluded itself, that the unreconciled tries to destroy every possibility of reconciliation.

Thirdly, in conceiving the good as an individual and universal harmonization, the criterion for openness must constantly be aware of the unreconciled, excluded evil that is inevitably within every good welcome: good and evil are actually the transcendental elements of the choice and coming-into-being of an alternative, continually created by the visionary power at the origin of culture.

Finally, the Good can be taken as the intrinsic ethicity of culture, i.e. as the act of originating alternative visions: as the unity of good and evil in the Good of the power of vision and of alternatives. This way of understanding the Good does not mean suppressing distinction and opposition, relative to circumstantial good and evil, nor understanding the Good as the Whole that has always contained them, but as the unfolding of a creative imagination that stretches towards the infinite arc of universal and individual harmonization. In this sense, the Good is both transcendent and the symbolic eschatological fulfillment of culture.

Here theory and practice meet: truth must be created in a tremendous effort to overcome the unreconciled for another form of reconciliation.

Will victim and hangman then be reunited, beyond all justice, in the supreme, conclusive injustice of universal eirenism? The truth leaves victims and hangmen to their mutual, unsubstantiated truth; it consigns them to their recognition and implicit truth. But it does not dispel their tragedy, it does not escape their unconsolability. It must find a new path, for which the recognized need for interdependence permanently calls forth the desired need for a comprehending reciprocity that reconciles the free self-realization of each person with the agreement and consensus of the others. Such inspiration certainly recalls some noble, utopian genealogies, from Buddha Sakiamuni to Isaiah, to Socrates, Jesus of Nazareth, Al Hallaj, Erasmus, Kant, Fourier, Baha'Ullah, Tolstoj, Gandhi, Etty Hillesum, Capitini, Thomas Merton, the Dalai Lama, Thich Nhat Hahn, and an infinity of others, known and unknown.

"We will be friends with all beings and with all things," such is the wisdom of an American Indian saying. This communion is an eschatological reality; it is more than the original truth of freedom: it is the truth of the Good that has crossed the conflict between good and evil and has come out pardoning evil, and has thereby achieved freedom and truth in the harmonizing choice that includes and accepts disharmony, without denying or destroying it.

In this regard, Jesus of Nazareth's cross, and the wounds of his resurrected body are a paradigmatic mythologem[49] of the choice that testifies to the good that is inherent in accepting even the destructiveness of evil. This comprehensive pardon prevents evil from becoming victorious and occupying even the so-called "good's" place of meaning, i.e. the good that desires the destruction of evil and thereby unconsciously turns into evil. In this move, the cross becomes the Easter of Resurrection, the passage of freedom outside divisive evil's law of slavery.

The divisive essence of evil impedes every freedom because it does not let it be; it negates the alterity of that which is differently imaginable, the unfolding of freedom. Without one possibility cohabiting beside another, i.e. without a positive correlation of co-present alternatives, freedom does not exist. If freedom does not choose this co-presence, i.e. the good, it destroys itself and thereby loses every possible truth.

The Good is a result of freedom; it reaches its truth and metaphorically retraces its origins in order to affirm itself as its condition, where the good no longer appears as a choice of freedom, but as the goal of freedom that manages to express its abilities. In this sense we might even say that freedom follows the necessity that pushes it onwards.

---

[49] Here the term "mythologem" does not mean the negation of historicity, even if we are dealing with a history transcribed in the "sacred language" of the Jewish tradition. On this enormously complex topic, see Carlo Enzo, as well as his as-yet-unpublished monumental work on the Gospel according to Matthew.

"Originary truth" means that it continues to occur, not that it stands at the beginning of a process. This communion continues to occur in every attempt to affirm and positively effectuate a universal reconciliation. It does not wish to negate its infinite negations. We know and accept the history of a freedom that is unable to reach itself because it believes it can affirm itself against others. All the same, we will persevere whenever possible in effectuating the alternative that creates a space for including conflict and negation without identifying itself with them, obstinately distancing itself from them instead, and calling for their differentiation.

The adventure of culture acts on originary freedom through given constraints, inventing in nature a new nature through its nature; in this it is but the vital dimension that reaches itself. If, recognizing itself, it itself wants, its freedom shows that the truth of its existence has the interdependence of inter-intra-being as its destiny and necessity, and this truth, joined to itself, must be taken up as a task: to show that one is a cohabiting communion in the planetary ecumene.

III Philosophy and Existence Today: Philosophical Practices between *Epistéme* and *Sophía,* by Luigi Vero Tarca

1 The *Epistéme* (Science) as *Sophía* (Wisdom)

Why are there no "true philosophers" today? Is it possible to practice philosophy as an experience of wisdom at the present time? In our culture, the figure of the philosopher as a "master of life" or a "wise" person has nearly disappeared, and trying to resuscitate it seems antiquated and pathetic. If by "philosopher" we mean the classic type of man who orients his own existence towards a wisdom based on truth, we might be tempted to declare that our civilization is bereft of philosophers. And yet even today our culture is rich in philosophy, it is full of "professional" philosophers (How many philosophy professors are there in Italy alone?). And we basically still think of philosophy as something that fundamentally deals with wisdom. And yet it is a fact that we are short on "philosophers;" indeed, we lack even the claim to being philosophers. And there is more. This lack is quite far from being considered a defect: professional philosophers avoid being introduced as wise. Moreover, almost all of them would denounce as out of place and absurd any philosophy teacher who claimed to act as a spiritual guide or master of life to his or her students.

From this we can see that the gulf between the actual professional philosophers (above all philosophy teachers) and the traditional image of the wise philosopher is due more to structural than to casual causes, i.e. this gulf depends upon theoretical reasons rather than contingent circumstances.

In effect, this situation depends in large part on the fact that a particular conception of wisdom and knowledge has predominated in our civilization. Ultra-schematically, this conception equates knowledge with rational – i.e. "logical" – thought, and more properly with "epistemic" thought. Philosophy is the experience that clearly and explicitly manifests a conception for which *sophía*, or wisdom, is equated to the *lógos*, i.e. to discourse, and in particular to rational discourse, paradigmatically exemplified by the *epistéme*, or science.[50] Wisdom – or that which guides people, who are constantly threatened by evil (the negative), towards the good (the positive), and so to salvation – coincides with thought, and more precisely with scientific thought: wisdom implies sticking to the true knowledge of the *epistéme*. We might say that philosophy arises from the fact that men have been "stunned" or seduced, or "blinded," if one prefers, by the light that emanates from the knowledge of the "exact" sciences (arithmetic and geometry above all, then astronomy and music). But why has science exercised such a strong fascination on people?

The epistéme *as objective knowledge of the laws of reality.* The contents of scientific discourse (*lógos*) are the laws[51] of reality. The law is universally valid, i.e. for all the individuals of a group; it expresses what remains identical in a series of different single cases and is therefore common to all of them. The universal[52] thus represents what is essential, and in this sense what is binding,[53] for all the different elements of the group. In as much as it is the essential de-

---

[50] While the term "science" essentially recalls a typically modern conception of knowledge, the word *epistéme* evokes the original meaning of the Greek experience of philosophical knowledge.
[51] The meaning of *legge* is connected to *léghein*, and thus to *lógos*. [*Legge* is the Italian for "law." – *Translator's note*]
[52] The *uni-versus* (turned to form a whole) gathers together a variety of determinations, almost turning them into a unity, a whole.
[53] The word *vincolare* comes from the Latin *vincire* (to bind, tie). See also the meaning of the Greek *léghein*, whence *lógos* (discourse, reason). [I have translated the adjective *vincolante* as "binding," as that is its meaning – *Translator's note*]

termination[54] of the totality of a certain group of individuals, the universal is determined, and yet it also holds for all of the elements that it embraces. Thus the law constitutes a particular determination (and we could also say an *object*), which nevertheless holds for the individual cases in a group. Scientific thought is therefore *objective*, in the sense that it is both universal and determined.

The law also has the particular characteristic of not being a banal, undifferentiated repetition of a monolithic object. On the contrary, it expresses the link among different elements, i.e. a *connection* among distinct determinations: the basic law stating that a body's velocity is determined by the force that is exerted upon it links two elements, velocity and force. In as much as this connection remains identical in all of the single, individual cases contained in the universal law, the law expresses the binding connection (the necessary nexus) that obtains among distinct elements and among different determinations. It is precisely the necessary nexus among different elements which constitutes an essential trait of epistemic thought.[55] The nexus between A and B is necessary (I will speak in these terms for the moment, and will later take up this fundamental topic) when negating B amounts to negating A as well; whatever is undeniable is necessary. The necessary nexus is what defines logical implication, which not coincidentally took on an absolutely central role in the development of Western philosophy, at least from Aristotle to Hegel. This consists in the fact that, given a determinate element, *another* element that is *different* from the first, *necessarily* follows.

But there is another peculiar, and particularly important, aspect to scientific thought: namely the fact that its laws obtain for infinite groups of elements. For example, a simple mathematical equation ($y=2x$) holds for all numbers – which

---

[54] For example, an essential trait in man is the faculty of reason, which thus necessarily belongs to all humans. Or at least this is so if we stick to the ancient definition of man as the reasoning animal (*lógon échon*).

[55] In mathematics, the product of multiplication necessarily follows from its operation (12x27 necessarily gives 324); in logic the conclusion of a syllogism necessarily follows from its two premises ("All men are mortal; Socrates is a man; therefore Socrates is mortal"); in geometry a triangle necessarily has the property by which the sum of its internal angles is 180°; and so on.

are after all infinite –[56] just as a theorem from geometry concerning triangles (the sum of their internal angles is 180°) holds for all infinite possible triangles. What is extraordinary about this state of affairs is that scientific thought seems to allow *determinate* knowledge of something that holds across an *infinite* extension. The infinite series of "objects" that we know through science is in some sense already given *here and now*, if only formally.[57]

Science therefore is a system[58] of necessary connections among an infinite number of different elements, which are nevertheless perfectly determinate, in the sense that their definition is already definitively formulated here and now – even if the whole series of such elements, which is only formally present, can never be exhibited in its entirety. In as much as the content of scientific law is perfectly determinate, we can easily call it a sort of object, and therefore we can call scientific knowledge objective: it presents the law that expresses an infinite, universal condition as a given (an object). Thus epistemic knowledge seems to allow man to know *here and now* something that holds *for everything and forever*; in this sense we can easily say that scientific knowledge provides a priori knowledge.

In as much as the content of scientific law is both a necessary and infinite determination, we might say that epistemic knowledge is the essential knowledge of reality. If the properties that it expresses are denied, unlike those that have been called "accidental," it fails the very nature of the entity to which knowledge refers. This is also why problems such as essence and definition have suddenly become central to philosophical thought. For example, knowl-

---

[56] Once a numeric value has been assigned to x, then the value that y assumes remains automatically, equally fixed for all of them. And the group of values that we can assign to x is infinite, just like those for y: if $x=2$, then $y=4$; if $x=6$, then $y=12$, and so on.

[57] For example, within the confines of Euclidean geometry we can state with certainty that the sum of the internal angles of all infinite, possible triangles equals 180°, even if we have obviously encountered only a finite number of triangles. And yet, what we are talking about is perfectly determinate, even if it holds for all triangles, i.e. for an infinite series of elements.

[58] *Syn-hístemi* = com-position. See the discussion further on of philosophical com-position. See also *syn-títhemi* (synthesis).

edge of the essence generally makes rigorous (deductive) reasoning possible;[59] precisely because the essence points out those traits which permit us to assert universal propositions truthfully.

It is well known that it is rather difficult to determine concretely what the essences of things are; nevertheless (and this is the "lightning stroke" or *coup de foudre* of epistemic knowledge at the moment when philosophy emerges) there is no doubt that it is legitimate "to attempt the essence,"[60] for science is a concrete example of essential knowledge. And if essential knowledge exists, then *a fortiori* (all the more) it is possible.[61] But if such a knowledge is possible, then all that we need to do is understand concretely *how* it is possible, i.e. what method will allow us to gather essences. It is no coincidence that the question of scientific method is still central to philosophical debate today. In the meantime, the existence of science permits us to say one thing: universal, objective, necessary knowledge is possible.

The "salvific power" of the epistéme: Man's agreement with reality. By why should such an epistemic knowledge be "salvific"? Why should it be taken as a model of wisdom, of *sophia*? To begin with, we might say that this depends upon the fact that knowing the laws that govern nature allows men to live in harmony with reality. Moreover, in as much as life constitutes a happy (positive) experience for men, when it is led in harmony with nature and with other men, epistemic knowledge becomes an essential condition for a successful, fulfilling life: scientific knowledge is essential for human existence to realize itself completely. It is precisely in as much as it succeeds in identifying the laws that govern reality that the human animal succeeds in "knowing" its surroundings, and potentially the whole earth. Thanks to such knowledge, man's

---

[59] It is because man's essence is mortal that we are able to perform the syllogism above regarding Socrates' mortality.

[60] This expression is Galileo's, but he uses it to show that traditional research into essences must be abandoned in favor of knowledge of formal structures such as mathematics and geometry.

[61] *Ab esse ad posse datur illatio*: From the fact that something *is* (exists) it is legitimate to conclude that it *is possible*.

natural context, his habitat, becomes a *civil* world, and the entire universe becomes a *cosmos*,[62] characterized by repetitions that man experiences, and governed by rules and principles that he partially knows. And the possibility for man to live in harmony with all that there is springs precisely from his knowledge of reality as an ordered totality. And this is so because when man knows the laws that govern reality, he is here and now capable of acting in such a way as to be able to live according to "universal" reality, and thus to enjoy its benefits and avoid its risks.

The "salvific power" of the epistéme: Infallible foresight and efficient action. The most immediate, obvious example of the benefits that man derives from the scientific knowledge of reality is that the *epistéme* permits what we might call "truthful foresight." Or in other words, knowing the necessary connections among different determinations (what I called "logical implication" above) permits us securely to infer, from one determination that appears in "actual" experience, a different determination that is present in another part of reality. For this reason science constitutes the paradigm of a secure and even infallible foresight, in as much as it is necessary and undeniable. In human life, foresight has a fundamental, omni-pervasive role, but given our limited experience, knowledge of what lies beyond it is constitutively problematic, and therefore continuously exposes itself to the risk of being contradicted by facts, and thus of turning out to be false.

Well, human understanding can find a secure hold in scientific knowledge's necessity: thanks to universal, necessary knowledge we are able to know here and now what reality is like in a place and time different from ours. Our human experience is constitutively finite: it is limited in space and subject to continual variation; thus in as much as it is essentially de-termined and partial, it always points to something further, to a whole that transcends it. This originary finiteness poses a great problem, in that it exposes us to the risk that what lies beyond our current experience may arrive on the scene, shaking and threatening

---

[62] The etymology of this word tells us that it indicates something ordered.

its positive traits. In its universality, scientific knowledge allows single individuals to go beyond (*metá*) the physical (empirical) dimension, turning towards what lies beyond and embracing the whole. And in this sense we may say that knowledge is originally *meta-physical*.[63] It therefore allows man to overcome the risks connected to his finiteness, and thence the unpredictability of existence, which men tend to consider negative, since we cannot know if something unpredictable will be a good rather than an evil. But even the mere fact that something contains *the possibility* of turning out badly constitutes a negative trait. And by guaranteeing infallible foresight, necessary scientific knowledge allows men to escape this risk, if only partially.

The advantage of truthful foresight as guaranteed by the *epistéme* becomes immediately clear if we consider that it is precisely upon this that man's capacity to attain his ends through the use of adequate means is founded.[64] Infallible foresight is therefore the premise of any efficient working upon reality, and thus of any fruitful action, which eventually includes individual efforts to control natural phenomena, and in particular dominating hostile forces. The *epistéme* seems to be the necessary condition for man to *control* reality *securely*. In its undeniability, necessary knowledge guarantees that man will act in-contrastably, and therefore also in-vincibly; it guarantees secure efficiency, and with it absolute strength.

In as much as being able to succeed in one's actions is indispensable for man's satisfaction, we might say that epistemic foresight is the essential condition for a fully satisfying human experience; as we can see today in particular with regard to technics (*téchne*), which is the realization of the *epistéme*. But achieving one's goal seems to be the necessary condition for accomplishing any good. So it seems that the *epistéme* constitutes the singular good that par-

---

[63] From this point of view it again seems correct to consider truth as "uncoveredness," i.e. as *alétheia* in the sense of *a-létheia*, "non-concealment."

[64] Assuming that B necessarily follows from A, we know that if we are able to "realize" A, then we are sure that we will also have realized B. If we now call A the means and B the end, we can say that epistemic knowledge permits and guarantees efficient action, for it guarantees that the end B necessarily follows from the means A.

tially represents the foundation and condition of possibility for accomplishing *any* other good. And as such, it is the indispensable condition for man's full self-realization, at least in so far as this implies giving oneself goals, projects and so on. It is precisely this peculiar characteristic of epistemic knowledge that has enchanted – or *bewitched* – Western thinkers. They perceived the possibility of having at their disposal a knowledge that concerned the real world,[65] while still being a priori valid: what we know epistemically here and now cannot be contradicted by anyone at any time. The decisive and particularly fascinating aspect of the *epistéme* which has allowed it to be equated with *sophia* is that it possesses the extraordinary, particular advantage of guaranteeing the accomplishment of any good in general.

The "salvific power" of the epistéme: Free agreement among men. But there is another feature of universal, necessary knowledge that takes on a particular value and meaning for man. Precisely in as much as it concerns the aspects of reality that remain common in all different situations, it holds for all men, independently of their particular situations; epistemic knowledge is thus binding for all subjects. This circumstance has vastly important consequences concerning one's behavior with respect to other men, for, in as much as he or she sticks to a truly universal knowledge, the individual is authorized to establish something here and now that holds for all other people and forever. So, in that it is binding for everyone, universal knowledge guarantees that all knowing subjects – i.e. all men – will be in certain agreement, at least as long as they stick to that knowledge. From this perspective, then, it follows that scientific knowledge guarantees agreement among men.

I must stress moreover – and this aspect too is fundamental – that what I am talking about is *free* agreement, precisely because the condition that forces all men to recognize the same truth and to arrive at the same result is different from the constraint and imposition that can be obtained through violence. It is rather the fruit of man's free recognition of the same objective, universally

---

[65] We might recall that "geometry" comes from *ghê* (earth) and *metréo* (measure).

valid truth. Man's free recognition of scientific truth is emblematically exemplified by the episode in Plato's *Meno* in which Socrates leads the young slave to the discovery of the truth of a theorem from geometry by asking him simple questions. The message is all too clear: scientific truth is independent of anthropological differences (of age, role, social status, instruction, etc.); it is spontaneously accepted by all those endowed with reason. But then, in as much as one defines man as an animal endowed with reason (*lógon échon*), scientific knowledge becomes a domain in which the peaceful unification of all men can take place. In the eyes of a wise Greek, science represents a domain for free, universal agreement among men: the ability to achieve a universal yet free condition makes the *epistéme* present itself as the domain in which a harmonious unification of men can occur. There are at least two fundamental reasons why it is entirely obvious how this is a decisive feature of human well-being.

In the second place, from the moment that this unity is in fact realized in scientific knowledge, i.e. through free acceptance, we can say that any action that is in harmony with the universal is just, if by this term we mean precisely that which is valid for *all* individuals, in the sense that it *has value* for all of them. From this perspective conformity to epistemic knowledge constitutes the *justification* for human action. Thus, by guaranteeing the "justice" of our actions, necessary knowledge legitimizes our "political" choices, i.e. the particular decisions which hold *for all others* even *without their explicit recognition*, even though they are taken by *someone* in a *particular situation*. In as much as they are universally valid, these choices turn out to be incontestable, and therefore incontrastable, and precisely for this reason *legitimate a priori*. Thus on the basis of epistemic knowledge, it becomes possible for a single person to make decisions that are not only destined to succeed and therefore to achieve his or her aims, but that turn out to be binding for all other human beings as well. At the same time, from the moment that they will *surely* be accepted as valid by all reasoning beings, no one will oppose these aims; in fact everyone *will have* [*dovranno*] to acknowledge their value, given that it is universal.

The connection that develops among men who possess epistemic truth is therefore different from one that is obtained through external constraint, a despot's impositions for example, as was often the case (in the eyes of the inhabitants of the Greek *póleis*) in the Eastern world. It is completely obvious how important this trait is for realizing a satisfying human life. In fact in as much as the individual sticks to truly universal knowledge, he can be sure that others will always approve his action. And as such it will guarantee him the essential goods of security and peace, saving him from the risk of the extreme evil of violence among men, especially through war.

Knowledge appears as *dike* in the epistemic logic as I have been discussing it, i.e. as justice; in its capacity as objective truth it takes form in law (*nómos*), and then in the just right (*ius*) that governs the city and human life.

Thanks to the two traits I have been discussing (the efficient control of reality and the free unification of men), the *epistéme* seems to be the fundamental motor for humanity's emancipation, i.e. for realizing a fully satisfying human experience. Human well-being (satisfaction) in fact requires that we be able to control reality (which must appear predictable, and therefore usable towards the promotion of our life), and that we do so harmoniously.[66] So as long as our actions conform only to epistemic knowledge we are certain of acting efficiently and justly. We could say that the epistemic word is both *true* and *good*.

This circumstance can be highlighted more formally if we begin by considering that un-deniable necessity coincides with a particular yet essential feature of the positive, which consists precisely in being the negation of the negative, and thus the guarantee that the positive occurs. In order to understand this point, let us begin by observing that the etymology of the word "necessity" already reveals the equivalence of the meaning of "necessary" and of "negation of the negative." It in fact literally (*ne-cedo*) indicates something that does not give up (*non cede*)[67] in the face of an adversary's attack; if this attack is a form of *negation*, and thus "ceding" to it constitutes something negative, then not ceding represents the negation of a negative: necessity is the negation of the

---

[66] From a slightly different point of view, we might say that this second trait (free agreement among men) constitutes the possibility for individual men to "control" even the actions of other humans, which is the decisive aspect of reality.

[67] It does not retreat, get out of the way or move; it is immobile and immutable.

negative, and it is for this reason that it coincides with the un-deniable, for the un-deniable [*in-negabile*] is of course the non-negative [*non-negativo*]. But the negation of the negative is an essential feature of the positive: Is health, which is positive, not necessarily the negation of illness, which is negative? Is knowledge not non-ignorance, wealth not non-poverty, and so on? Is the good not generally speaking the exclusion – and hence in some sense the negation – of evil?

All the "positive" aspects of epistemic necessity express the double negation at work in necessity. The necessary is in fact *in-tangible*, in as much as tangibility implies a negative transformation, i.e. the negation of what is "touched;" therefore it is also *non-contra-stable* and *im-mutable*, in the sense that it cannot turn itself into its own negative.[68] If the universal's positivity consists in its being the positive in its relation (of distinction) with the negative,[69] necessity is the universal's moment in which the agreement among determinations is *guaranteed* to occur, at least in the sense that its non-occurrence is excluded or negated. Thus necessity is a particular feature of the positive which consists in guaranteeing that the positive will occur in the positive's capacity as the negation of the negative, and then, in as much as the non-negative is an essential part of the positive, in guaranteeing the positive's capacity *tout court*. It is precisely the conjunction of the two features (*guarantee* [of the] *positive*) that explains how our civilization has been led to equate *epistéme* with *sophía*, and especially with the apex of *sophía*, which permits this latter to present itself as the *guarantee* of the good, towards which wisdom claims to guide humans.

The philosopher's wisdom. But there is one particular trait that warrants our attention. What confers knowledge-value upon epistemic knowledge is its ob-

---

[68] In its immutability, the object of the *epistéme* is eternal, objective, inter-subjectively valid and thus subjectively binding. And given these traits, necessity is incontrastable [*non-contra-stable*], it is that which cannot be discussed [*non-contro-verso*], and hence is incontrovertible [*non-contro-vertible*]. The undeniable, the necessary, thereby generally constitutes the objective universal, and thus the determinate infinite: the objective in-finite is un-deniable.

[69] A characteristic of the universal is that its different determinations (which, in their quality as such, *could* have a relationship of mutual negation) are identical, and hence harmonious.

jective (universal, necessary) character, i.e. its independence from all the aspects of reality by which men could be in conflict with reality and with other men. Here I mean the aspects that concern not only subjective inclinations, personal tastes, individual desires, but also moral values and conceptions of reality, at least in so far as these points of view are influenced by "particular" (historical, geographical, environmental, cultural, ethnical, etc.) factors. This means that the "salvific" value of science depends on the fact that its principles exclude any personal and evaluative element of experience, at least in so far as this entails a subjective, individual, arbitrary and arguable component.

A sort of paradox begins to emerge where the *epistéme*'s "ethical" value, which consists in being the principle path for promoting human existence, depends on its non-valuational, non-value-based and impersonal (im-personal, non-personal) nature: *science's value to man resides precisely in its "denial" of its evaluative, existential components.*[70] Epistemic laws are "salvific" in that they are in-contrastable, but they are salvific in as much as they are freely acknowledged by all, and this in turn depends on the fact that they are *neutral*. Their neutrality further implies that they are impersonal, and to some extent amoral, at least in the sense that they are bereft of any moral pre-judice that claims to stand before the absolute value of "objective truth."

It is worthwhile to stress how the "positive" traits I refer to above as belonging to scientific knowledge depend upon its impersonality, i.e. by the fact that it constitutes a negation of the individual's actual needs, where the individual is understood as a complete, living, concrete person. It is only in so far as men deny their own instincts and individual, subjective inclinations that they necessarily agree. And so it is only in as much as they are "scientists" that it is impossible for them to disagree. Therefore only science's impersonal knowledge, through its impartiality (im-partiality), can be objective, and as such, have an immediate inter-subjective value.

---

[70] Galileo's distinction between primary and secondary qualities provides a clear, meaningful example.

Clearly this entails a certain sacrifice on the part of the individual. But the sacrifice is worth performing, for, on the basis of what we have seen above, renouncing the complete satisfaction of one's needs is not the same as bending before the arrogant, alien power of other men, but only before the power of reason, which men themselves are able to understand and control through their free intellect. We could say that the sacrifice of one's own individual freedom is in turn the fruit of an individual's free choice. The renunciation that scientific knowledge demands of the concrete individual is a worthwhile sacrifice. In fact, it is to his greatest advantage, for there are values that are so important for men (such as collaboration with others and peaceful relations) that it is reasonable to sacrifice even a good part of one's "personality" and "individuality" to them. Thus it is wise of men to have confidence in such a unifying, harmonizing power, even if doing so entails a significant renunciation.

These considerations help us to understand why a civilization that takes the *epistéme* as the paradigm of knowledge in general, and then as a model of knowledge, ends up producing a type of sage who is very different from the traditional "wise man." From this point of view, the "true wise person" is obviously someone who adapts to the objective truth of the *epistéme*, rather than someone in search of individual perfection. Or perhaps it would be better to say that personal value is directly proportional to the individual's ability to abstract from his own, single personality and to adapt to the rules of the (theoretical, technical, political, etc.) apparatuses that are the fruit of epistemic knowledge. Meanwhile, the value of his practical action will depend upon its ability to conform to the true theory. And in so far as practice is the alternative dimension to the one that is subordinated to theory, it will somehow remain erased from the wise person's horizon.

For the same reason his behavior will be characterized by a sort of singular immorality (im-morality), in that it will have to stick exclusively to the final value of truth, even when doing so forces it to sacrifice what might subjectively seem to the individual to be "moral" values. For this reason, from the moment that its own ethical value is guaranteed by the "objective truth" of epistemic knowledge, to which alone it is obliged to answer, wisdom that adapts to im-personal epistemic knowledge is characterized by a sort of in-difference and even by irresponsibility (non-responsibility) with respect to individuals' vital, concrete needs (including those of the subjective agent). Far from constituting a defect of this interpretation of wisdom, distancing oneself from personal involvement constitutes its essential value: the meddling of arbitrary, variable, subjective elements would in fact amount to a turbulent interference in the pure objectivity of scientific knowledge. This is why in our civilization those who cultivate philosophy are so far from the traditional figure of the wise person. Far from representing a lack of wisdom, this signifies a precise mode of understanding wisdom, which equates *sophía* with the objective, impersonal knowledge of the *epistéme*.

2 Philosophy as the Total Extension of Scientific Knowledge

Philosophy's program. Philosophy is born from the enormous impression that the splendor of scientific truth makes on men, and it constitutes a plan for emancipating humanity that is based on the *epistéme*: we must adopt scientific knowledge as the foundation and method for the universal self-realization of a satisfied, peaceful humanity.

But the *epistéme*'s "salvific" value obtains only if scientific knowledge succeeds in being total. As long as knowledge remains partial (i.e. relating to one part), it risks turning into its opposite, for in such a case it cannot be applied to the *other* part that it does not control. It therefore risks being contradicted by that uncontrolled part, and this situation would strip it of the universal, necessary characteristics that confer its peculiar value upon it. This obviously holds for its ability to control reality, but it also holds – perhaps more so, or at least more intensely – for the emancipating aspect of scientific knowledge. For, if scientific knowledge only concerns a limited domain of existence, and is thus "partisan," then the power that it unleashes, concerning its ability to control reality, can be used *by one part* of humanity *against another*; it can be used by some men to dominate and subjugate others.

Given that by definition men can disagree about what the *epistéme* does not control, they may disagree on how to use the formidable instrument of scientific knowledge. In other words, in so far as science is partial, it appears as instrumental knowledge, which as such is far from guaranteeing that it will be used positively rather than negatively for all humans. According to this second hypothesis, scientific knowledge's "justice" turns into injustice, and science goes from being a path toward emancipation to a tool for man's damnation, at least for the damnation of some men, but then, in the end probably for all. The guarantee that, though it is amoral (in the sense that it does without all moral values that are not the truth), even scientific knowledge has a fundamental ethical value depends upon the fact that it has universal value. But if this nature comes up short, then its "ethicity" turns into the greatest immorality, i.e. a full-fledged *negation* of moral values. If epistemic knowledge does not succeed in being total, then it entails the extreme risk that its (positive) value turns into a (negative) disvalue, that its plan for emancipating men transforms into an intensification of violence and submission.

In so far as philosophy is meant to lead humanity towards the good by means of epistemic knowledge, its program must be to extend this knowledge to every domain of existence. This effort to "totalize" epistemic knowledge therefore has two sides: on the one hand, it attempts to "valorize" every aspect of human experience by putting it under the control of the *epistéme*; on the other, it represents the achievement of the only condition for which the subjugation of human existence to scientific knowledge constitutes something positive rather than negative. Thus the development of philosophy consists in transforming every aspect of human existence according to epistemic laws.

Emerging from its admiration for the scientific disciplines that already existed at the time of its birth (in the first place, the "exact sciences" such as arithmetic and geometry, and then astronomy and music), philosophy extends itself in two directions: first it "subjects" every domain of scientific knowledge to epistemic criteria; next it "justifies" this operation by introducing the notion of values to scientific knowledge. Thus, precisely because philosophy presents itself as the horizon that is able to make the *epistéme* the heart of human freedom, it must turn its gaze precisely on those aspects that define man's humanity, i.e. ethical values as well as the principles of social and political cohabitation. It is no coincidence that philosophy's first great form, i.e. the Socratic/Platonic dialogue, puts questions regarding the nature of the good, the just, the sacred, and so on at the center of philosophical, dialectical thought.

If we confer the name "truth" upon epistemic knowledge, we can then say that philosophy is meant to extend the truth limitlessly. If we then call "rational" that which takes only the truth as valid, then we can state that philosophy is meant to extend rationality to all questions.

The limit of the philosophical knowledge. For the form of rationality that considers an action valid when it conforms to epistemic truth, a position is valid only if it is able to justify itself based on a law, or to show that it necessarily derives from universal principles: rational choice has a valid *foundation* in truth. But when such rationality is extended to everything, limitlessly, it runs into a peculiar difficulty.

From the philosophical point of view, *all* positions must be justified, thus *every* position p must be justified. Yet this seems impossible, for any position is justified by itself or by a position that is different from itself (which I will call j), but in both cases, we find ourselves in a logically unacceptable situation. In the first case we will have a *circulus vitiosus* (vicious circle), or else a *petitio principii* (petition of principle): a position is justified through a demonstration that *presupposes* the validity of the position that it is meant to justify. In the second case, on the other hand, we are confronted with a *regressus in indefinitum* (infinite regress) which prevents us from effectuating the justification. In fact, in this case justifying p potentially implies a position that is different from itself, i.e. its justification (j). But then we will have to justify this new position as well, and this justification must in turn depend only on itself (in which case it would immediately fall into a vicious circle), or by p (in which case it would once again fall into a vicious, if mediated, circle, in as much as p would justify itself by way of j), or else by a position that is different both from j and p, and is therefore a new position (which I will call j_1). It then becomes clear that we would have to demand a further justification of this new position, producing a similar situation to that of our starting point, which opens the way for an infinite development.

Thus philosophy's task seems impossible to perform: it cannot arrive at a conclusive justification, because it ends up either in an endless, foundational regress, or in a circular foundation. Philosophy's plan seems destined to fail because it demands that only justified positions be accepted as valid, i.e. that no position whose value is simply presupposed can be accepted. And from what I have said up till now, it turns out that every justification implies a presupposition; in fact, the justification for any position presupposes the value either of the position itself or of another position. If we are unable to overcome this difficulty, or limit, of philosophical discourse (its inability to found itself), we will have to acknowledge that the philosophical project has failed.

The undeniable as philosophical principle. From a certain point of view, a great deal of philosophy is the attempt to overcome this fundamental difficulty. I will now try to present what I believe to be the most concise, efficient way of tracing the path that philosophical thought takes when attempting to reach a foundation that escapes both endless foundational regress and vicious circularity.

This difficulty can be overcome by showing how there can be positions that by their very nature need no justification, for they *cannot be denied*, from the moment that *even their negation would be forced to affirm them*; they are thus *undeniable*.

We saw earlier how justifying a position (B) means showing that denying it amounts to denying another position (A) that we took as true: justifying B on the basis of A means showing that B is undeniable as long as A obtains. But philosophy needs a total foundation, and thus an absolutely, unconditionally undeniable position. Well, a position such that even its negation would be forced to affirm it would be absolutely undeniable, for its negation cannot exist. Indeed, in its normal conception, negation is *definite* precisely because a thing (A) cannot be the thing it negates, and conversely, A's negation cannot be A (non-health cannot be health, the good cannot be the non-good, and so on).

And so, if we stick to this definition, we must say that if there is something such that even its negation, should it exist, would belong to it, then this something is undeniable, precisely because there can be no negation of it.

We could present this circumstance (in which a position is affirmed even by its own negation) as the position's *philosophical justification*. And this justification is perfectly rational, for it is based solely on "epistemic" notions, such as the true and the false, and not on someone's authority, or on empirical or extrinsic presuppositions. At the same time, it is *conclusive*, for it eludes both infinite regress and the vicious circle. It eludes the former because it reaches a point where the need for demonstration stops, given that no further position is assumed as true; it eludes the latter because it does not presuppose its value: in fact it simply presupposes its nature, or its meaning, i.e. the fact that by its intrinsic constitution it cannot be denied. Such a singular justification can do without presupposing the truth of any position; all that it presupposes is simply the presence of a position with only its meaning, and not its validity. It does not presuppose the value of any position, whether the one that is being justified, or any other. It seems that we have found a way to overcome the proposed difficulty, and as such, to reach a conclusive, philosophical foundation.

Let me take an example. I believe that the simplest, clearest way to exemplify this situation relates precisely to the notions of negation and the negative. It is easy to see how these notions possess the extraordinary property I mentioned above. In the case of negation, for example, it is clear that its negation (the negation of negation) also belongs to the thing it negates (i.e. negation); the negation of negation *is* that which it negates; it is negation. And so the affirmation that the negation of negation is negation is surely true. The same obviously holds for the notion of the negative, which I will now take as the paradigm for our examples, as it has an advantage over the notion of negation in that it overcomes the gnoseological limit implicit in the latter expression. Thus we can say that from the moment *the negative of the negative is in its turn negative*, there can be no negation of the negative, and therefore *it is undeniable*.

Generally speaking, this allows us to say that we have found a method, or criterion, for identifying philosophically true positions: those positions that are undeniable in the sense that even their negations are obliged to affirm them. From a slightly different point of view we can say that the negation of undeniable positions is self-negation, for their negation, precisely in that it denies itself, affirms what it is meant to deny. It follows that propositions such as "the negative exists," "negation exists," "the false exists" and other similar ones seem necessarily (undeniably) true, because they turn out to be true even when they are false: if negation, the negative or falsity did not exist we would have a situation in which the negation of negation, the negative of the negative, the falsity of a proposition that affirms the existence of the false would exist, and so on. Conversely, one could say from this perspective that the negations of these propositions cannot be true, for it is the very fact of their being true which makes them false.

Thus, as I said before, there exist rationally justified positions, i.e. that can be justified using purely logical, rational arguments, which do not thereby require us to presuppose the validity of any position. We seem to have resolved our problem concerning the possibility of philosophy, and therefore of an undeniable, self-founding principle. I call this type of justification *élenchos negativo*, for on the one hand it employs what traditional philosophy has called *élenchos* (or "elentical procedure"),[71] and on the other it makes this procedure more rigorous by wrapping it around the notion of the negative.

This approach is negative in at least two senses. In the first place, it takes a negative content (negation, the negative, the false) as undeniable; in the second place, its truth consists in a position that denies some other position. This negative *élenchos* can be described as follows: *the negative is undeniable because the negative of the negative is negative*. Thanks to it, we seem to have found a domain of undeniable truths and a method for identifying them.

---

[71] I must here refer the reader to the works of Emanuele Severino.

3 The Truth as Freedom with Respect to Necessity

The truth as pure difference. The above position concerning the negative (i.e. that the negative is undeniable, since even its negative is a negative) is nevertheless much more aporetic and paradoxical than it at first seems, for the undeniable becomes the negation of the negative that should not exist, given that the negative is undeniable. Let me explain.

"Undeniable" ("un-deniable") literally means "not deniable." But that which is not deniable cannot be denied (for if it were denied, then it follows that it is deniable[72]) and therefore it cannot be negative (for the negative is defined as that which denies and is therefore itself denied,[73] and thus all that is negative is also denied); thus the un-deniable must be non-negative, and so the negative of the negative. So here the un-deniable itself is just that negative of the negative which should not exist, from the moment that the negative is undeniable. Thus the same negative, precisely in its being un-deniable (i.e. non-negative), is the negative of the negative, thus the negative of itself. Thus the undeniable, in as much as it is the negation of the (undeniable) negative, is the negation of itself, and in turn the negative, in as much as it is undeniable and therefore the negative of the negative (non-negative), is the negation of itself. Both the undeniable and the negative are what they deny; they are their own opposites: the negative, in so far as it is un-deniable, is non-negative, and the negative of the negative, in so far as it is the negative of something, is negative. In short: the un-deniable, precisely in as much as it is un-deniable, is deniable, and the negative, precisely in as much as it is un-deniable, is the negative of the negative.

Philosophical truth now seems to have been turned upside-down, and the resulting situation seems paradoxical and extreme. Philosophical truth's conclusive justification leads to the negation of the same notion that it is based upon

---

[72] If a thing *has* a certain property, it goes without saying that it *is possible* for it to have that property.

[73] That which denies (let's call it A) denies something (its negative opposite), and is thus denied by its opposite; this holds even for the case where the opposite is simply equivalent to the negation of A.

(the un-deniable). Philosophy arrives at the complete dissolution of itself. It seems that we have fallen into the most extreme, irresolvable contradiction. And in a certain sense this is so, but it is this very circumstance that allows us to perceive a way out of this mess, even if it is easy to see that the way out will be equally extreme and paradoxical, as we shall now see.

The un-deniable is the negative, but at the same time it is the negative of the negative, thus the undeniable-negative is both negative and non-negative. Consequently, in as much as the negative is un-deniable, it is and is not negative.[74] But at the same time, and for the same reason, it is and is not non-negative.[75] But precisely in as much as the undeniable-negative is that for which it is the negation (its own opposite), it is *different* from the negative in as much as this latter *is not* that for which it is the negation. Therefore, for the same reason, it is *different* from the non-negative as well, in as much as this latter in turn *is not* that for which it is the negation.[76]

Here we are therefore dealing with a mode of being that is *different from the negative in general,* i.e. (and this remark is fundamental) *from both the negative and the non-negative.* But equally fundamental is the further observation that this something-other-with-respect-to-the-negative-in-general must as such be different both from the non-negative and from any entity that, while being a *tertium* with respect to the negative and the non-negative, nevertheless continues somehow to be negative with respect to something,[77] as happens particularly when we define this *tertium* as something that *is neither* the negative nor the non-negative.

Through the figure of the undeniable-negative, an alterity that is *totally* different from the negative appears with respect to this same undeniable-negative.

---

[74] It is negative in as much as the negative *is negative*; it is not negative in as much as *it is that of which it is the negative.*

[75] It is non-negative in as much as it *is un-deniable*, and it is not negative in as much as *it is that for which it is the negative.*

[76] That which differentiates the undeniable-negative from the negative, in as much as this latter is not that for which it is the negative, is something different from its being non-negative, in as much as even the non-negative remains defined as that which is not that for which it is the negative.

[77] And it would be so simply by being the *negation* of something.

We thereby perceive a meaning of differentiation for which the difference be-tween two entities must be distinguished from every form of negation. What emerges is a difference between difference and negation which we might call *pure* or *mere difference*,[78] precisely because it distinguishes itself from every form of negative and negation,[79] and therefore from the negation of that difference which is negation.

The undeniable-negative thus consists of two aspects or moments: n_1 con-sists in *being negative*, and particularly in that particular negative which is the negative of the negative; n_2 consists in being *different from the whole negative*, and therefore also from that particular negative which is the negative of the negative, i.e. the non-negative. In so far as n_2 differs from the totality of the negative, we may call it *pure different*, because it is the aspect of reality that differs from the whole negative. From this we can speak of *pure determination* as well, in so far as "determination" is all that is different from something, and in our case the "pure" differs from the totality of the negative. In this sense we can thus speak of pure being, in so far as the pure determination is, and also of pure positive, in so far as the pure determination is posed and is therefore something positive. But then, in so far as the pure different manifests itself in the figure of the undeniable, i.e. in that which is a priori universal, it presents itself as *pure universal*.[80]

From the philosophical point of view the present situation has an extremely important trait. In as much as the undeniable-negative – which from the phi-losophical point of view is, I hasten to remind the reader, necessity – is the pure

---

[78] I mean "mere" in its etymological sense of "pure, neat, true and proper."

[79] From the moment that all that which entails negation is negative, every negation implies a negative, and every negative has a trait for which it is negation.

[80] I prefer to say of the pure universal that it is "pure with respect to the negative" rather than use expressions such as "pure of the negative" or "immune to the negative," as these more easily give the impression that the pure is something that *is not* the negative, i.e. something that some-how entails a negation. The expression "pure with respect to the negative" helps to understand that the pure differs from the negative even in its relation with the negative, i.e. even though it is *in the presence of*, or *before* the negative. The same is true for expressions such as "free of the negative" and so on.

determination that distinguishes itself from the negative in general, it distinguishes itself from itself as well, given that even it is a negative, in as much as it is an undeniable-negative. But we now know that this difference must distinguish itself from every negation as well. Thus it must also distinguish itself from all that is the negation of necessity, as well as from that particular form of negation that is the negation of the identity between necessity and the pure determination, i.e. between n_1 and n_2. Thus we must say that there is at least one sense in which the two moments coincide, while remaining different.[81] We see here that peculiar relation for which a determination differs from itself, but in such a way that this difference is purely compatible with its (the determination's) being identical with itself. This means that there is also a meaning of difference and identity for which two determinations can coincide.

The pure universal as the transfiguration of necessity. With the figure of the pure universal, philosophical "totalization" is complete: the pure universal is a determination that appears as the aspect of the undeniable-negative that is different from every negative and is therefore different even from the particular negative of the undeniable, i.e. epistemic necessity. Philosophical justification is therefore completed through what we might call the "the transfiguration of the undeniable into the positive," i.e. the purely positive transfiguration of necessity and the negation of negation.

To wit: the end of rational justification consists in showing the undeniability of the position it is trying to justify. This means that that justification's "positive" end consists in showing that a determinate position is untainted by negation, by the negative. This strategy, extended everywhere by philosophy, bumps into an essential limit: when it tries to free itself from the negative in general it appears inefficient and contradictory, because the negation of the negative in general reproduces the negative rather than freeing itself from it. We must therefore pursue the end of freedom with respect to the negative in a

---

[81] We might say that they coincide at least in the sense that they *are all one*, as a body part is all one with the body, though it is in some sense distinct from it.

different manner, one which as much succeeds to the extent that it differs from the negation of the negative too, and differs from it in a way that differs also from the negative in general.

In this sense we may say that the pure universal is the transfigured accomplishment of the undeniable: it arrives at the same end as that which the undeniable pursued, but it does so differently. The undeniable differs from the negative only through this transfiguration, and is therefore free from the negative in general and the un-deniable, at least in so far as differing from something amounts to being free from it.

In so far as it is the transfiguration of the undeniable, the pure universal represents the "positive" accomplishment of the elenctical foundational procedure, for this time the *élenchos* presents itself as different from every negative, in contrast to the "negative" which leads to the identification of the undeniable with the negative. In so far as the pure universal is the transfiguration of the undeniable, it appears as the fulfillment and transfiguration of epistemic, objective knowledge. Full-fledged philosophy appears then as difference and freedom from epistemic necessity, and thus from objective knowledge as well. But, as we have already seen, this freedom-difference must be distinguished from every form of the negation of epistemic objectivity. It is purely universal in so far as it succeeds in positively relating with even undeniable necessity, objectivity and the negative.

Philosophy achieves its end by distinguishing between the universal that is a priori valid and the undeniable; the difference between them is given by the pure universal, which is a priori universally valid precisely because it differs even from the undeniable. Philosophy frees itself from necessity, but this freedom arises from epistemic logic itself, which means that it is present in necessity as well. This essential, double relation of positive, coincidental difference, subsisting between the pure universal and necessity, is fundamental. On the one hand, full-fledged philosophy is the expression of *true* necessity; on the other, this "true necessity" is wholly other with respect to necessity (*il tutt'altro della necessità*),[82] in so far as it is negativity, and hence is freedom from necessity's negative side. Full-fledged philosophy is the universal freed from all negativity, and hence from every necessity.[83]

It is for this that we can say that philosophy expresses "true necessity," by which we mean something that is essentially *other* with respect to necessity. All the same, when speaking of "other" with respect to necessity we must keep in mind that it is the meaning itself of alterity which is involved, for that for which necessity is other than necessity still belongs to necessity. We tend to think that that which is other than something is so (i.e. other) in so far as it *is not* the something than which it is other.[84]

Well, in our case we are faced with a singular situation, for the other that exists along with necessity (the un-deniable) is different from both the traits that define necessity and everything that *negates* these traits. It is other than everything that is defined by necessity's traits, and other than everything that *negates* them; it is other than everything that exists within the negative (including the undeniable), but in the same sense it is other than that which is foreign to it, if this foreignness is the negation of something.

From this new perspective a new, unheard of and transfigured sense of alterity emerges: all of the terms in question (identity, alterity, difference, etc.) undergo an essential transformation of meaning. Moreover, the meanings of all

---

[82] The formula "tutt'altro di," which in Italian is at the limit of grammatical correctness, is meant to indicate an alterity differing from the excluding and negative one with respect to the whole. [I have translated this formula as "wholly other" in order to keep the notions of both otherness and wholeness – *Translator's note*].

[83] On the other hand, as we have seen, this "alterity" with respect to the negative and to necessity is still the result of necessity's rigorous thought, when taken to its logical limit. Thus this alterity to some degree *coincides* with necessity.

[84] It may even be internal to the something, but the traits that make it other than the something are different from those that make it belong to the something. For example, an "elephant" is other than an "animal" even though it is "included" in the class of animals. But what makes it an animal (for example, the fact that is alive) is not what makes it other than an animal, in so far as it is an elephant (for example, the fact that it has a trunk, which not all animals have). In our case, however, the reason for true necessity's otherness with respect to necessity is the same as that which makes it necessity, i.e. its undeniability. Thus, this "other" with respect to necessity (true necessity) is also something that coincides with necessity.

words now undergo an essential transformation, because we are moving from a domain in which one meaning arises *in opposition* to every other meaning (*omnis determinatio est negatio*) to one in which one meaning differs positively from all other meanings. We could perhaps say that due precisely to this essential transformation of meaning, philosophical truth is alterity with respect to alterity.[85] This alterity is alterity with respect to itself, in as much as it too is negative.

We can therefore say that philosophical truth (philosophical discourse) is a witness to the wholly other with respect to necessity, and thus also a witness to freedom with respect to the negative and to necessity. Thus, taking advantage of the similarity and difference of the meaning of "obligation" [*dovere*] with respect to "necessity," we could express the positive difference between necessity – as the negative – and "true necessity" by saying that that which (in truth) *must* [*deve*] obtain is the differentiating from the negative, or the freedom with respect to the negative. Through the word "must," the sentence says that freeing oneself from necessity is a form of necessity, but it is a *positive* necessity, "true" necessity. Furthermore, we could point to the "ethical" component of this perspective by saying that, from the moment that *eluding the negative is possible*, what we must do, or we have to do [*ciò che* si deve *fare*], is free ourselves from the negative, and from necessity, in so far as this too is an expression of the negative.

4 The Philosophical Principle from the Search for the Undeniable to Nihilism

Figures of necessity. Thus far, our considerations might seem wildly abstract with respect to the concrete, living fabric of philosophical experience. I conse-

---

[85] The situation of "true necessity" is analogous to that which occurs when we say that "true revenge is forgiveness," or that "true victory in war is to make peace," where the specific identification (forgiveness, peace) of a concept (revenge, victory) is in some way an alternative to what it is also meant to exemplify.

quently feel obliged to show how these "poor" formulations are really able to represent the topical moments of Western philosophical thought.

I have said that the principle of Western philosophy is undeniable elenctical foundation. This is fully confirmed if we pay attention to the absolutely key role that the so-called "principle of non-contradiction" has played in our philosophical tradition. In the first place because the negation of undeniable propositions is self-negation. But from the moment that self-negation is a contradiction, this means that, in so far as philosophical propositions negate contradictory self-negations, they are defined by being the negation of contradiction: philosophy's principle is non-contradiction. In the second place because the principle of non-contradiction can be presented as an emblematic example of undeniable discourse for it is founded elenctically. Moreover, it is hardly a coincidence that Aristotle's establishment of this principle, especially in the fourth book of his *Metaphysics*, constitutes the first clear, explicit formulation of the process of elenctical foundation. As Aristotle has it, the principle of non-contradiction is undeniable, for in order to deny it, one must give a determinate meaning to its negation by opposing it to the principle itself. This shows how it can also be called a "principle of opposition:"[86] every determination means what it means through its oppositional difference to every other determination. If by "opposition" we mean the negative difference between two determinations (negative at least in the sense that it is the negation of their identity), then we can say that the undeniable principle of meaning and being is the opposition among all determinations.[87]

Moreover, this principle is simply the fulfillment of preceding philosophical thought. If Parmenides had already defined truth as the *opposition* between being and non-being, and therefore as the *negation* of non-being, in the *Sophist* Plato maintains that the truth of being consists in the fact that every "be-er" [*essente*], in being *héteron* (different) from being ([*essere*]; i.e. the fact of being, or the whole of being) , is to some degree its negation, at least in the sense

---

[86] Or principle of difference-negation, or even of determination-negation.
[87] From this perspective contradiction means equating two determinations, precisely because their identification negates their difference.

that it is the negation of its identity with being. This is how he commits "parricide," violating "father" Parmenides' prohibition of stating that non-being is, precisely because every be-er is non-being, in so far as it differs from being.

After Plato, the truth of being is the affirmation that every "be-er," every determination, is negation, at least in the sense that it is the negation of its own identity with every determination from which it differs, and thus with every other determination. The *true law* of being is the relation that pits every "be-er" against every other "be-er" and against being itself. It is this notion of opposition among determinations that Aristotle identifies, in the fourth book of his *Metaphysics*, as the crowning notion of philosophy.

The fact that philosophical thought is founded on a notion of opposition allows us to understand Western culture's essential ambivalence. Western culture has so often turned *sophía*, which is meant to guarantee the greatest positive, towards *negative* phenomena, which has today led to a radical nihilism, i.e. the experience of that extreme negative which is nothingness. This occurs because on the one hand necessity is the positive (we have in fact seen that it is the feature of the positive by which the latter is the negation of the negative), but on the other it transpires that, from the moment that the undeniable is the negative, it is precisely *the negative* which acts as the *positive* principle of human freedom.

It follows that promoting positive epistemic necessity amounts to encouraging the negative that is inherent in it. And this explains the tragic reversals that our culture's knowledge is up against, not to mention the nihilistic result to which it leads. This nihilism is nevertheless "necessary:" in so far as the undeniable manages to resist every possible negation, the philosophical method consists in the negation of all that can be negated; only that which resists this effort can legitimately be considered philosophical truth. So it is natural enough that the end result of this process of universal negation is that negation (the negative) itself is the only undeniable element that remains.

But this self-negative nature, explicitly manifested in nihilism, is a constant of philosophical thought, for this latter largely consists in overthrowing all the determinations that it has itself identified with the undeniable absolute, which in its turn is destined to act as the last foundation of knowledge and as the guide of human existence.

A particularly emblematic figure of this proceeding is the God of Christianity. Saint Anselmo's so-called "ontological proof," for example, consists of an impressive logical move by which he irrefutably demonstrates the existence of a perfect being (God) through an argument that derives God's existence from the mere *notion* of God: a being greater than which nothing can be thought (the definition of God) must exist, for if it did not, then the something larger (more perfect) would be thinkable, which would be precisely the same "thing" (or "be-er"), only provided, above, with existence. But in this case God would no longer be a being greater than which nothing can be thought, and thus would not be God.

Rather than getting into the "hornet's nest" that Anselmo's extraordinary invention raises, I will merely point out its fundamental trait: the existence of God is an absolute philosophical truth, because it can be shown through reason alone (*sola ratione*) such that even someone who wished to deny it (the atheist, or *insipiens*) would be forced to affirm that God does not exist, precisely in order to deny it, but this entails thinking the notion of God (a being greater than which nothing can be thought), and hence of assuming that it exists, and thus of recognizing the truth that he intended to deny.

Thanks to this absolute truth, philosophy achieves a very strong unity of the whole of reality, which now turns out to be entirely governed by an omnipotent, rational principle: the God of Christianity is a God-*lógos*, the creative-destructive principle of reality and thus the reason that incarnates itself in the world, leading it to salvation. In so far as God is both a speculative principle that is able definitively to found philosophical knowledge (Augustine, Anselmo, etc.) and the force that effectively transforms the world (Hegel), it exemplifies the paradox that the largest, most radical transformation of the world takes place in the name of that which is immutable and eternal.

Another figure with an analogous role is that of the modern subject, emblematically represented by Descartes' *cogito*. This also constitutes an undeniable principle, for it is elenctically foundable, for only someone who is thinking can say, "I deny that I am thinking (*cogito*)," thereby achieving what he or she claims to deny, and invalidating the negation. Kant's transcendental Ego in large measure derives from this *cogito*. By way of German idealism, this transcendental Ego leads to Hegel's absolute Spirit, which in turn reappears in the materialist dialectic of Marx's revolutionary praxis, and has ended up today as the omni-transformational force of a technological and politically organized structure.

It is precisely this reference to technnics which allows us to perceive another typical figure of the philosophical absolute: modern science. Through it, nature in reality reveals that it is written in mathematical signs, as Galileo put it. If God is the infinite, creative power of all aspects of reality, the man after Galileo, the scientist, is he who has the knowledge to decipher the language of creation. The advent of modern science leads to considerable acceleration and intensification of the philosophical-epistemic program: Galilean science becomes a paradigm for every other science.

But there is more. Modern science is pushing towards the qualitative leap of techno-science, or as philosophy has traditionally called it, "technics" (*téchne*). The conjunction of the theological principle (God as the supreme force and absolute principle of the transformation of the whole world) with modern science (the human knowledge which mortals possess, but which is nevertheless able to penetrate the deepest secrets of the whole of nature and creation) in a certain sense puts man on the same level as God the creator. Western man is resolutely moving toward a scientific, epistemic knowledge that is able to guide the limitless transformation (creation, destruction) of the whole of reality. What we must understand, and what the contemporary thought of Heidegger, Severino and others is based on, is that technics constitutes a great experience of truth, which in a certain sense represents the apogee of the philosophical parabola.

To summarize this complex problem, if we call "truth" the guarantee of the correspondence (agreement) between theory and reality, then the correspondence can occur in two ways: either we develop a theory that is capable of reflecting the necessary, undeniable, immutable facets of reality, or we transform reality in such a way that it conforms to the dictates of theory. The Western philosophical, epistemic parabola consists in progressively moving the philosophical strategy of truth from "theory," which aims to identify the "objective" elements of reality, towards "technological praxis," which transforms everything that is mutable in such a way that it conforms to our "projectural" grids.

But a further, and equally important, figure of the philosophical "absolute" develops in the objective structures destined to organize, control and produce the social life of men "in a just manner." I mean of course the institutional and administrative organisms of the modern state, culminating in contemporary ethical states, and in the political, bureaucratic organization of current social life.

The negation of all undeniables in contemporary thought: The relativization of necessity. All of the figures in play with a claim to the absolute (the unconditional, elenctically founded undeniable) have ended up being questioned by negative, epistemological logic: in as much as any undeniable is the result of the method of universal negation, it ends up succumbing to that negation. From this point of view, philosophy, i.e. the attempt to establish the absolute principle of reality, describes a parabola of the progressive abandonment of the conviction that it is possible to identify such an entity, i.e. a truly undeniable, and therefore truly immutable, entity.

Western philosophy generally negates all undeniables, but our age has truly set about "rendering (or settling) accounts" with every claim to establishing an absolute undeniable. Contemporary philosophy (from Nietzsche to Wittgenstein, from Heidegger to hermeneutics and positivism) has attacked the foundations of the ideal of a philosophical, epistemic knowledge, i.e. of a total, definitive knowledge, based on an undeniable principle.

Obviously, there are numerous variations on this theme, but here I will summarize this complex question by formulating it in the following manner: in so far as everything is finite, *everything is relative to a determinate context*, but then everything varies according to its context, and therefore *everything is deniable*, precisely because anything that is some way at a certain moment can at another moment become the opposite of what it was before. This applies in particular to the value of truth in propositions. Thus every truth is relative; it is in fact "in relation" to a context; it thus varies according to its context and therefore turns out always to be falsifiable and revocable.

It is important to understand that the variability of context involves all elements of reality, even so-called "fixed," objective ones; these too vary at least in as much as they are in relation with the aspects that vary.[88] In short, we can say that if something varies, then everything varies, but if everything varies then there is nothing invariable or immutable. Therefore, given that variation does exist, there are no undeniable truths.

And this holds for mathematical and logical propositions as well, for variability implicates even meaning. Contemporary thought accentuates how the same meaning (and thus concepts, ideas, etc. as well), far from being an immutable, untouchable entity, changes according to the words used to express it. To paraphrase Wittgenstein's famous formula, which has played a key role in dismantling the fixity of meaning, we could say that meaning varies as a function of language games, and thus of anthropological practices and human forms of life.[89]

But if even meaning is subject to change – however slowly this may occur, and however imperceptible it may be to the individual – then the truth of propositions that have traditionally been considered undeniable and immutable

---

[88] Let us assume that the two situations, S_1 and S_2, have a common element A, which is the invariable, immutable object of the situation. In that case, S_1 and S_2 would be composed of two parts: one that is identical in both and is therefore common (A), another that is different and therefore not common, which I will call B_1 for S_1 and B_2 for S_2. So we have $S_1=A+B_1$; $S_2=A+B_2$. But when A is in relation to B_1 it differs from A when it is in relation to B_2, thus the A in S_1 is in fact different from the A in S_2. Thus, the A in S_1 is really A_1, while the A in S_2 is really A_2. Thus we have $S_1=A_1+B_1$, and $S_2=A_2+B_2$, and the common, identical element has disappeared. It is clear, furthermore, that the same problem would turn up infinitely if we attempted to distinguish the part of A_1 that remains constant from that which is invariable.

[89] We could say that the meaning of an expression varies as a function of each of its individual applications. I take "function" in its mathematical sense: in $y=2x$, variation in the value of x leads to variation in the value of y, and similarly, in our case to every new use of a linguistic expression there corresponds a new meaning.

(mathematical, logical, metaphysical ones)[90] is also variable and thus revocable. Precisely because the reason these propositions are held to be incontrovertible is that one need only consider their meaning in order to establish their truth; one need not examine reality experientially. Yet this is only possible if one assumes that at least this meaning is fixed and immutable. Obviously we could perhaps continue to say that these propositions are undeniable, but that would now simply mean that they are so in the same way in which the rules of a game that we have decided to take up are undeniable.

In short, to say that logical, mathematical propositions are undeniable means only that we have *de facto* decided to withdraw them from discussion. And moreover, not even this protects their meaning from change, for meaning can unexpectedly bump into different, even opposing, yet entirely legitimate, interpretations. In short, through the medium of language, even the "metaphysical" domain of ideas and meaning is led back to the world of empirical, becoming reality. But if not even "ideas" are immutable any longer, then there can truly be nothing left, not even "undeniable" propositions, that escapes natural, factual reality: everything therefore is mutable, everything is revocable.

The negation of all undeniables in contemporary thought: The supremacy of the practical, existential interpretative context. So, every "objective" truth, every proposition or law, is relative to its anthropological, pragmatic context; its objectivity is determined against a background of a system of reference which stands behind the same formal law. Thus the system of reference cannot be the content of a discourse, precisely because in order for the content to be content, it must *presuppose* the background, which *as such* can never become the content of an utterance. Here we bump into the limits of language: uttering, and hence every utterance, has an essential limit. It cannot represent its own form as an objective fact, because a fact is objective only in so far as it stands fully before the subject, which cannot otherwise know and "capture" (under-

---

[90] For example, "2+2=4," or "Either it is raining, or it is not raining," "Bachelors are not married," "The part is included in the whole," and so on.

stand) it. But if the object stands before the subject, then it is clear that the subject can never objectively know the background to any knowledge, and within which alone an object can be formed.

If the object of vision is produced by the "act of focusing," which thereby throws something else out of focus (the background), then it is obvious that the structure *qua* structure cannot become the object of the act of focusing. At the moment when it becomes the object, it loses its status as background. Obviously, knowledge's "gaze," which first focuses on one aspect of reality, bringing it into the foreground, and thus leaving the background hazy, can then turn toward the background; thus we might concede that nothing in principle is excluded from becoming an object. But what is impossible in principle is for all reality to become "an object" in one stroke and all together, precisely because the definition itself of "objective reality" implies the distinction between object and background.

The practice of "objectivizing" thus has an insurmountable limit, for every "fixed, immutable" object is only a "fixation" of ours; it is therefore in-the-becoming and variable as well, if for no other reason than that it is exposed to the variability of our decisions and linguistic practices. But if every truth presupposes a constitutive background, or interpretative context, then (following Nietzsche, and appropriating an authentic slogan of contemporary thought that has widely been hegemonized by hermeneutics) we could say that *everything is an interpretation*, and that for this very reason there is no absolute truth. In this sense, we could employ the term *interpretative context* for the structure that constitutes the limit of meaning of various objective knowledges. But the interpretative context, within which alone any objective truth is formed, is still within a *life practice*, which cannot be erased, without risking the loss of meaning of the theory itself.

Thus every theory presupposes a practical, existential background of meaning, which implies a value-based, moral, metaphysical system of reference. It is worthwhile to recall the importance of existential hermeneutics, which begins with Husserl's assertion that scientific knowledge always develops within the concrete, vital, human world (the *Lebenswelt*, or "life-world"), and moves the philosophical discourse from essence (objective truth) to existence (for example, Heidegger's *Being and Time*), and therefore turns the analysis of existence into an interpretation that permits us to approach the form of philosophical truth that is largely absent from objective knowledge and missed by it.

The negation of all undeniables in contemporary thought: The rejection of truth, in as much as truth is seen as violence. All of this has relevant consequences from the ethical and practical point of view. If there can be no undeniable objectivity, then anyone who claims to possess philosophical truth is deceitful, overbearing and finally violent, even when this process begins with self-deception. For, far from soliciting universal agreement (in accordance with the definition of epistemic knowledge), the claim to transforming the world in the name of something that cannot exist becomes an imposition upon everyone of a particular, determinate, and hence arbitrary way of interpreting life and the world. Thus it turns out in particular that, far from being the premise of his or her full realization, the aspects of the *épistéme* that characterize the "sacrifice" of the individual instead lead to his or her damage and disintegration.

It is for this reason that contemporary thought presents itself largely as a peremptory, definitive rejection of any claim to transform reality philosophically. Claiming to transform reality on the basis of philosophical truth implies choosing between being among the weak who are naive enough to believe in good faith that they possess truth, and being deceivers who know that they do not know truth and nevertheless exploit the word's fascination in order to impose their own will to power on the world; the latter are obviously violent hypocrites living in bad faith. And history, particularly recent history, seems to confirm this position unflinchingly: the claim to constructing a world that is based on divine truth has led to intolerant, violent forms of theocracy. Yet on the other hand, even the attempt to construct a world based on the truth of words such as "liberty," "fraternity" and "equality" has led to cruel, merciless dictatorships which, instead of relieving the world's ills, have intensified its dangerous, violent elements.

The negation of all undeniables in contemporary thought: Anti-dogmatism, criticism and nihilism. This great work of negating all undeniables takes on two principle forms. The first is more "urbane," or "civilized," and shows philosophy today as a critical, anti-dogmatic stance that reveals its remote elenctical origin by the fact that anyone who wishes to critique it would have to assume a critical stance.

The second, more disquieting form is extreme nihilism, whose elenctical, philosophical origins are clear, for it is the necessary outcome of assuming that only the negative is undeniable, as this latter is strictly speaking the only "thing" that is reaffirmed even when denied, and hence concludes that *nothing is the ultimate truth.*

This outcome is a rigorous consequence of Western thought, which we might describe as a progressive "distillation" of the absolute negative at which it arrives.[91] This outcome obviously has a clearly onto-logical side, which says that reality consists in universal becoming, i.e. in all things' tumbling into nothingness, and an epistemological side, which says that nothing is [the] undeniable truth, and that the fundamental criterion of knowledge is fallibilism. But this also has a practical, "technical" side for which all things are created (produced) and destroyed: everything can be transformed, manipulated, projected, destroyed and produced.

The negation of philosophical truth, which at first sight obviously appears as a dead-end for philosophy, also turns out to be its authentic accomplishment: the self-realization of philosophy consists in its suicide; its full realization consists in refuting itself. It is in fact philosophy itself that affirms that it is impos-

---

[91] If at the beginning of philosophical thought all ideas are immutable (Plato), with Galilean and Newtonian science the "necessary" conceptual apparatus is narrowed down to the system of mathematics and geometry. And with the logical, mathematical researches of the late 19th and early 20th centuries, the epistemological foundation further narrows to a handful of logical, conceptual notions. Analogously, the scientific a priori progressively shifts from content to method: the true "immutable" (unmodifiable) of scientific thought is less a group of "real" contents than the methodological apparatus which guarantees its truth, independent of how this method is interpreted, i.e. whether as hypothetical deduction (Galilean science), or induction (empiricism), or logical formalism, or as logical fallibilistic corroboration, etc.

sible to realize the philosophical dream. One of contemporary thought's central moments is the scientific, epistemic demonstration that the philosophical dream is impossible. Gödel is perhaps the most emblematic of this turn, but Tarski, Wittgenstein, Russell and others are also important. They in fact rigorously, scientifically "demonstrate" that philosophy's epistemic dream cannot be realized because it is contradictory.

Let me briefly explain. Philosophy's theoretical system is defined in the first place by being epistemic, scientific, non-contradictory, and in the second by being *total*, universal. Well, Gödel and Tarski's studies literally mathematically demonstrate that these two criteria cannot be satisfied together: if the system seeks consistency, then it cannot be total; if it seeks totality, then it cannot be consistent.

At this point, philosophical thought has found itself at a crossroads, dividing thinkers into those who choose non-contradiction and therefore science, and hence renounce metaphysics and totality, and those who renounce logical coherence in favor of totality and thus develop non-conceptual, non-logical, but rather symbolic, poetic approaches. If we call the first option science and the second wisdom, then we can say that we have arrived at the point where *epistéme* and *sophía* separate, i.e. at the end of philosophical experience, which consisted precisely in their union.

The philosophical question today. Thus the type of philosophy that chooses wisdom against epistemic knowledge attempts to free itself from logical, scientific, technological necessity. Schools of thought and speculative paths that are otherwise vastly different solidly agree on this score. One need only look at the path that leads from Husserl (particularly *The Crisis of European Sciences*) to Heidegger's re-reading of Nietzsche (and to his "imposition", on philosophical thought, of the problem of technics), then to Gadamer (who proposes an alternative to technical, scientific truth), and finally to contemporary hermeneutics.

On the other side, the philosophical perspective that begins with the so-called "scientific conception of the world" manages to question all the established points of epistemic knowledge, including immediate, sensory data on the one hand (thanks particularly to Popper), and the incontrovertible principles of logic on the other (Wittgenstein), and hence critically to relativize the scientific stance itself (Feyerabend).

It is also significant that important contemporary hermeneutists are interested precisely in the figure of "liberty," understood as that which is able to free man from necessity.[92] The "critical" stance of contemporary thought, from Heidegger to Severino, is very important in this approach with regard to technics, taken as the contemporary emblem of epistemic necessity.

Thus contemporary philosophy's primary concern is to provide a different philosophical truth (wisdom) from that of the *epistéme*. For this reason, it has begun to reintegrate the philosophical study of psychological, religious, spiritual, political, and other questions concerning human existence, but avoid the "scientific" methods that had been typical of the preceding period. Philosophical discourse has once more begun to deal with the problem of wisdom, and to rethink concerns that had been crushed beneath epistemic necessity: personal, practical and moral concerns, and even metaphysical, religious ones and generally speaking sapiential ones.

But the situation is hardly simple or calm: knowledge that merely rejects the *epistéme* would signal the end of philosophy, understood as the strict union of science and wisdom; moreover such a rejection would be profoundly antinomian, in that it would be the rigorous consequence of precisely the philosophy that it attempts to negate. In effect, if this new form of knowledge develops by separating itself from or opposing the *epistéme*, or in other words, if it limits itself to rejecting the philosophical aim of joining science and wisdom, then it risks aggravating, rather than resolving, problems.

---

[92] For example, the key hermeneutical approach of Luigi Pareyson. In this vein, other important contributions are those of *differance* (proposed by Gilles Deleuze, Jacques Derrida, and others), Italian so-called *pensiero debole* (or "weak thought" proposed by Gianni Vattimo, Pier Aldo Rovatti, and others), or ideas derived from hermeneutics (such as those proposed by Mario Ruggenini, Adriano Fabris, and others), or symbolism (such as that of Umberto Galimberti, and others), and even ideas that are quite far from hermeneutics (such as those proposed by Vincenzo Vitello, Massimo Cacciari, Carlo Sini, Salvatore Natoli, and others).

The situation becomes more dramatic if we realize that today epistemic knowledge appears as the mechanisms that dominate the world: science and technology, the military-industrial complex, the political, bureaucratic, administrative structure. Far from leading such a system of mechanisms to abandoning the *epistéme*, the failure of every undeniable limit favors liberating manipulatory power and thus the extraordinary intensification of limitless production and destruction of reality. This holds for scientific, technological planning and manipulation, for the revolution in political, organizational structures which are meant to govern men, and for the resulting rational, bureaucratic organization of existence. All of which leads to a disproportionate, and potentially infinite growth of technical, industrial structures as well as political and military ones, intent on dominating the whole of reality, both natural and human, which is headed ever more towards "rationalization" (Weber).

Once the domain governed by "necessary" laws (scientific knowledge, technological instruments, institutional organizations, etc.) has been separated from "philosophical truth," it continues inexorably and violently. Every attempt to bring it back under the control of personal and moral "values" is ineffectual or counterproductive, and so it always ends up in sustained, tragic forms of violence. And this occurs because if objective knowledge is unable to be total (i.e. philosophical), then its negative aspect, or the human sacrifice that it implies, is not only not compensated for by miraculous technological progresses, but in fact promotes their use in such a way that leads to complete, human disintegration, or even to genuine destruction in the name of the implacable needs of the apparatus. Thus as long as we refuse to reconcile necessity and wisdom, it is clear why the one continues inexorably in its potent, im-moral logic, while the other cultivates its "morality" impotently and ineffectually.

Unless we completely want to throw away everything that has to do with scientific, rational knowledge, which is obviously impossible in many ways, then in order to ward off this outcome we must continue to keep the philosophical project alive, even if obviously in a different way from the counterproductive, objectivist way. I would say that contemporary philosophy is largely in agreement on this point too. But the path is extremely narrow, because once we have sidestepped the "objectivist" solution, its "subjectivist" opposite appears equally problematical, i.e. the solution that finds a way out in the "subject's" control of objective mechanisms. First of all because objectivity had been taken as a value precisely because of subjects' observation of its "dangerous" nature, especially in relation to their inability to agree. To suggest now that we return purely and simply to individual, subjective instances means liquidating the problem instead of resolving it: the individual, taken as such, is the *problem* rather than the solution. In the second place because it grows ever clearer that the subject's attempt to submit the growth and functioning of objective mechanisms to his or her will is in practice a failure.

Here too we can identify a few fundamental reasons that lead to this outcome. Ever more clearly, the individual appears as a cog in a machine that discharges onto everyone its indifferent, irresponsible laws of functioning, which no one seems able to control any longer or to push in a direction that guarantees benefits rather than damage to men. More importantly, the development of technical, scientific, organizational potentialities has reached a point where, if only indulging in a certain peremptoriness and thinking in perspective, we can say that now even the same individual human is in turn a product of the technological mechanism rather than an external subject who can control it. It may seem then that the only practicable outcome is to harmonize existentiality and subjectivity with objectivity and impersonality. The last few decades in particular have witnessed a certain perspective gaining ground, one that imagines a progressive agreement for reconciling individual needs with the continual development of the "objective" world, renouncing any philosophical, truth-producing claim, and limiting itself to evaluating the given situation from time to time.

We could imagine a comprehensive progression that derives from partial adjustments geared toward occasionally improving every single, concrete situation, rather than from definitive, peremptory indications of truth. This truly is more or less what we are attempting to do; nevertheless the problem is that, if we lack a "regulatory idea," then any step we take risks leading us in the wrong direction, and the same is true for every possible correction that we wish to introduce. In fact, if we totally exclude any idea of philosophical truth, even these "small steps" always risk more clearly turning into a slow march toward the abyss rather than towards liberation.

Therefore we must keep the philosophical "project" alive, joining truth and good, science and wisdom. This, however, can occur only if we move beyond the impasse that thought creates when it falls into the *trap of the negative*, by which I mean a circumstance to which it seems impossible even to imagine *an alternative*, with respect to a situation that is defined by negative logic, (even though its very "negative" nature pushes us in that direction). For, in order to imagine an alternative to the negative, we would have to postulate a situation that was *not* negative, but this would be enough to make the situation negative, at least with regard to the negative situation to which it aims to be an alternative. Extreme nihilism represents a situation of this type, for it is the outcome of a search for the undeniable, carried out through the negative method of the negation of all that is deniable. Strictly theoretically, we have seen that we can escape this trap through the method of pure difference and the pure universal; now we must see what this means concretely for philosophy.

5 *Doing* Philosophy Today: Theoretical Practice as Com-position

Truth and negation. We will not free ourselves from the trap of the negative by outright rejecting the philosophical experience, but rather when our distance from necessity becomes a moment of that freedom from the negative in general which is the meaning of philosophy.

Thus post-epistemic philosophy must in some way take shape in discourse (the *lógos*), and must therefore "say" something, distinguishing itself from every position that finds truth in something that is *not* discourse. But in order for this utterance to distinguish itself from every revisiting of dogmatic, objectivistic truth it must distinguish itself from every form of negation. Obviously, such a philosophy can only develop within a domain for which saying and thinking do not necessarily imply negation. Full-fledged philosophical discourse distinguishes itself from every "negative" perspective, i.e. from every perspective that sees opposition as originary and unavoidable, and for which *determining amounts to negating*. In such a domain, *every difference is a negation*, if only the negation of the identity of two determinations; consequently every determination implies negation, and thus every affirmation contains at least one corresponding negation. Within this negative viewpoint, *the positive is defined by its (negative) opposition to the negative*.

Philosophy must question the principle that affirms that every determination is a negation (*omnis determinatio est negatio*), for as long as we assume that every determination is a negation, then even the content of philosophical discourse, which too is a determination, is a negation. It is only by questioning the principle of determination-negation that it can take any negation as a purely possible and eventual addition to a given position, and thus *succeed in conceiving of the possible*, which too is a determination, *as something different (even) from the negation of the negative*.

"Full-fledged" philosophical speech is therefore different from any form of negation. It is speech that "affirms" (for if it does *not* affirm then it becomes the *negation* of affirmation), and does so "philosophically," i.e. by speaking of the universal and of all that is connected to it (law, totality). But it speaks positively, and is thus an affirmation that differs from any negation.

The first criterion that we must adopt in evaluating philosophical discourse is therefore what I call "the negation gauge:" any negative proposition is immediately a philosophical problem. The philosophical stance takes every negation as an essential problem; it interprets every negation as the signal of a risky situation. Indeed, nowadays I am sometimes greatly embarrassed if I negate any proposition when doing philosophy, rather as I would feel if I let slip a swear word or a serious grammatical error when speaking in public. In other words, I see negation as a sort of serious act of "bad theoretical upbringing."[93]

---

[93] I have *at least attempted* to respect this criterion even in this essay. The reader must nevertheless keep in mind that when I refer, even indirectly, to "negative" discourses, I of course have recourse to negative formulations.

Yet the most instinctive, immediate approach to this risk, i.e. simply *rejecting* negation, leads to the same problem. We must therefore somehow create a discourse that distinguishes itself from both true negation and the *rejection* of negation. I believe that the correct stance for "positive" philosophical discourse is one where every negation appears in a context that strips it of its negative charge. For example, within full-fledged philosophical discourse, negation must appear as a sort of "quotation," on a different level from philosophical discourse; it can then appear inside philosophical discourse with a tone and a meaning quite different from the negative one. We might imagine something similar to a stage, where the "negative" (for example a murder, or simply an argument) is present, but within a fictional context of (ultimate) meaning, which from a certain perspective releases it of any real harmfulness. Another way of "presenting" this harmless negative is through irony, obviously understood in its positive sense, as I will explain later on when I take up this point more thoroughly.

Philosophical discourse that has been freed from negation is therefore purely affirmative with respect to all content and all things. By "positively" affirming everything, it affirms even negation, but in such a way as to defuse its negative charge, and this occurs when the negative charge is placed in a context that is able to deal positively even with negation.

Years ago, when I set out on this philosophical path, I tried to express what I might call a "purely positive" position, with this formula, "All discourses are necessarily true." Today I would probably say, "All discourses are absolutely true," precisely in order to rid the formulation of the "negative" charge implicit in the term "necessity." It is clear that this position (which I also called "omni-aletic")[94] is an attempt to make an affirmation about philosophy's central themes (such as truth and falsity) which surely differs from nihilistic or nega-

[94] The word is composed of *omnis* (everything) and *aletic* (from *alétheia*, truth).

tive statements, but at the same time distinguishes itself from "dogmatic" af-firmations that are also negative, though in a different sense.[95]

In pursuing this line of research, I found the key to the question in the *distinction between difference and negation*, and in particular in the effort to over-come the equivalence between difference and *the negation of identity*.[96] I have also had occasion to present this formulation as a sort of game, called "You said *no*." Yet it must be clear that whereas the game involved a simple exclu-sion of negation, this is itself negative.

This way of dealing with the negative, which we have called the purely positive transformation of the negative, is meant to achieve positively the same ends that epistemic philosophical discourse pursued through the "negative" method of negating the negative, which centered on the figure of the un-deniable (necessity).

Revealing a few key points in common should suffice. In the first place, a negation-free discourse accomplishes the need implicit in the principle of non-contradiction. Contradiction is the simultaneous affirmation and negation of the same proposition; thus a discourse that does *not* contain negations surely *can-not* be a contradiction. Obviously, truly to reach such an end we must free our-selves even from the negation that is implicit in proposing a discourse that *has no* negations, and this is precisely why we must move to pure difference.

But then all the other "positive" features of epistemic logic that negate ne-gation are purely positively fulfilled here.

To recapitulate, let us first look at the advantages implicit in epistemic knowledge. Given that it is undeniable (non-deniable) it is generally positive, as the negation of the negative. Consequently, as the negation of the negative implicit in mutability (or in variation), it is immutable (non-mutable). As such, it does not change with the variation of different situations, and is therefore

---

[95] Either because they have truth coincide exclusively with necessity ("Truth is necessity"), or because they still exclude, and therefore negate, the truth of other propositions, beginning with the negation of "dogmas" that are taken as necessarily true.

[96] In which affirming that determination A differs from B amounts to *denying* that it is identical to B.

indifferent (non-different). It thereby becomes a positive *in-dividual identity*,[97] in so far as it denies the relationship of mutual negation that can crop up between determinations.

The observant reader will have noticed that what I have just outlined above are in fact the defining characteristics of what is traditionally understood as Parmenides' being. This one-identical being is immutable and non-multiple. All of these traits can be expressed with the term "infinite (non-finite):" the object of epistemic, philosophical truth is the infinite, understood as that which denies the negativity implicit in the finitude of being. But precisely because it is directed at a non-mutable, non-different and non-finite object, philosophical knowledge is essentially an *impersonal* (non-personal) knowledge, which negates the negative aspects of the arbitrariness and subjectivity of existence. It is thus *just* knowledge, for it is impartial (non-partial, i.e. it does not "take sides"), and it therefore also has an ethical component, which however is essentially a negation of morality, and hence a form of immorality (im-morality), at least in so far as morality implies personal, existential involvement.

In as much as positive philosophical discourse is the positive transformation of the negative traits which the *epistéme* negates, it must rehabilitate them all, but such that they are free of the negative charge which was the reason for their negation by and exclusion from scientific knowledge. Moreover philosophical knowledge must be mutable, but its variation must be understood as being free from any negative charge. In particular this means that it must be imagined as being different from every form of negative variation; in particular its variation must be compatible with the stability of the identities that gradually develop.

Next, scientific knowledge must be multiple, i.e. differentiated, but this plurality of determinations must be such that their interrelationship is different from every type of incompatibility, exclusion and negation generally (including, and especially, the negation of negation itself). Thus philosophical speech must be *finite*, i.e. determinate (hence relative and finite). But given that this finitude must be free from all negativity with respect to any other determina-

---

[97] I mean the first term in its etymological sense of "undivided," or *not* dual, *not* multiple.

tion, then in the single, finite determination, philosophical knowledge must see and posit a relation to universal totality, in which all single finitudes mutually compose each other. Philosophical knowledge must then have a *personal* side in relation to im-personality, but such that it is different from what a single, individual existence opposes to other individual experiences.

The "personality" that positively transforms the negativity of im-personality *composes itself positively* with all other people. Analogously, philosophical discourse must ([*deve*]: has the duty) now express an essentially moral stance (as even the word "must" [*dovere*] implies), but in a different sense from the one for which this dimension opposes "objective reality."

If we now assemble all of these indications, we can say that "positively transformed" philosophy now constitutes an absolutely *open* knowledge that is *variable* in every single instant, yet also stable, and in some way eternal. Thus it is instantaneous and situational, i.e. it can adapt to each given situation, and hence is ever-new, inventive and creative. At the same time it also continuously reconfirms and permanently recognizes the same (*das Selbe*, rather than the *das Gleiche*, in Heidegger's terminology). Thus it is a precise, determinate and *living* knowledge, i.e. it is *existential*, and in this sense fully *personal* and *moral*, but at the same time it is complete, *total* and *whole* (thus free from the personality's dis-integration and scission). Thus it is in some sense *objective*, i.e. fundamentally equitable, and hence *just* and even *peaceful*.

Positive philosophy states the positive nature of reality; it states reality's freedom from the negative, and thus its wholeness, its integrality, totality and concreteness even in its absolute variability, plurality, openness and existential, personal concreteness. And it speaks this *in* and *of* the concrete situation in which it finds itself. We can sum up by saying that full-fledged philosophy is the *pure determination of the whole, or of everything.*

The self-limitation of philosophical discourse. A peculiar aspect of philosophy, understood as the positive transformation of the negation of the negative, warrants consideration here, namely its paradoxical, *self-denying* nature. We have seen that applying the method of the search for the absolutely undeniable, by way of universal negation, leads to extreme nihilism, and thus also to the self-denial of philosophical logic itself. Even this trait must now appear within philosophical discourse. And it can be positively transformed by distancing itself from itself, or in other words, by a sort of *self-limitation* and *positive self-overcoming* of philosophy itself.

Formally this means that in as much as universal, philosophical knowledge is itself a determinate, particular knowledge, it is a special moment of the whole to which it refers. Philosophical knowledge is a part that *speaks* the whole: the content of philosophy *is* the whole! Now, whereas in "negative" logic this immediately gives rise to a contradiction (the part is *not* the whole, and vice-versa), in "positive logic" this can be imagined free of contradiction. Philosophical speech is a positive distinction within its content between that for which it truly is the whole (the concrete whole) and that for which this concrete whole is itself a different determination from all others.

This singular circumstance has a peculiar trait, for which philosophical speech (concerning the whole) is a particular experience that contains even the relation that it itself, as a determinate reality, has with other determinations. This paradox is highly relevant from both the logical, ontological point of view (for its quite singular nature), and more importantly, from the ethical, practical, political point of view, for we are led to say that a philosophical position is truly complete only when its relations with "the world" are purely positive.

Philosophy thus appears at a distance from itself, in so far as it is negative. If however this distancing means sundering philosophy into to opposing camps (concerning negative and non-negative aspects), the operation would fail, because it would fall back into a negative logic. Therefore we must distance philosophy fully and totally, in the sense that it must completely encompass philosophy: it must self-differentiate itself totally and wholly from itself.

We may be able to form a preliminary idea of how such a thing is possible if we think again of irony, understood as a positive, rather than negative, distancing. It is surely important that this experience was so significantly present at the beginnings of Western philosophical thought, i.e. in Socrates' dialogic, maieutic practice.

Two points are of particular moment. To begin with, "philosophical" irony must be basically benevolent towards its target. One is often tempted, even when reading the Socratic dialogues (for example, the *Euthyphro*), and perhaps justifiably, to see irony as a way of poking fun at and deriding a false sage. Irony thereby becomes a particularly efficient form of "refutation:" like refutation, it too is a weapon, which is used to hit one's adversary "behind his back," rather than in a direct frontal attack. But by following at least some of the same Socratic indications, we ought to say that irony is essentially an instrument for care and healing, i.e. for *purification*. Thus it is very far from being an offensive weapon, and is rather more like a therapeutic instrument.

Philosophical irony must therefore be clearly distinguished from every form of sarcasm and even satire. Moreover, even when it is conceived as a means of purification, it becomes authentically philosophical when it is fully accepted by the person who "undergoes" it. Thus the "purified" fully supports the resulting purification; only thus does philosophical irony fully preserve the defining character of philosophical knowledge, i.e. that of expressing free acknowledgement.

Secondly, given that philosophical irony must be total and freely accepted by the same subject who undergoes it, it must direct itself toward the subject who is doing philosophy, and it must therefore be above all self-directed irony. Before it is used on others, philosophical irony must be turned towards the subject doing philosophy. But, it must be turned towards the philosopher *qua philosopher*: philosophy's "self-critical reflection" would be vastly incomplete if it maintained a dualism in which a philosopher could ironize about himself as a *non*-philosopher (for example, as someone subject to the normal fears of a common man, or as a violent being, as a creature plagued by the weaknesses of human nature, etc.).

We must therefore distinguish between self-directed irony and every form of indulging in its negative traits; irony must fully pervade even the philosophical side of human behavior. This means especially that taking one's own "truth" "lightly" is part of the philosophical practice. (You might say, "Look who's talking...." And, well, this would be a perfectly reasonable observation.)

Freeing oneself from a certain "seriousness" and "drama" of the philosophical word is an integral part of full-fledged philosophical knowledge. This is a difficult task, for philosophy deals essentially with the tragically painful aspects of existence, about which it often appears difficult to joke, as it is difficult to joke about "epochal" questions touching on human destiny. It seems almost impossible to "ironize" on these topics without seeming irreverent or offensive with regard to human suffering. And yet this is to some extent exactly what we must do: take ultimate, definitive questions "lightly" and at the same time "gracefully," always being aware of "how little is achieved" when philosophical problems are solved, i.e. when we have managed to "speak" philosophical truth. (On this point, I direct the reader to Wittgenstein's famous preface to his *Tractatus logico-philosophicus*.)

Thus we could sum up the philosophical perspective in a formula of this type: (s_1) "I always joke." This has the particular advantage of evoking one of the most typical and important propositions in the history of logical, philosophical thought, namely the so-called "liar's paradox:" (m_1) "I always lie." This proposition is self-contradicting (if it is true, then it is also false), so how can we use a proposition like s_1, which is so similar to m_1, to express philosophical truth? Well, precisely because s_1 represents the "positive" transformation of m_1: m_1 denies truth in general, and hence denies itself; by pointing out its ludic nature, on the other hand, s_1 limits the value of every utterance and hence of itself, yet this self-limitation does not necessarily imply self-negation.

S_1 is typically philosophical because it is truly universal, and as such it is self-referential and self-limiting, but it manages to do this without falling into self-negation, precisely because irony (the joke) is a form of distancing which differs from the negative one. For example, in so far as philosophical discourse must guarantee people's full self-realization, it risks sounding presumptuous and arrogant, especially when it is forced to take itself as an essential condition for that self-realization. At the same time, if it refused its task it would cease being philosophical discourse. Self-directed irony probably allows us to hold on to the philosophical claim, and to some extent, its truth, but it also allows us to ripen our awareness of how the philosophical experience is only a tiny light in the heavens of all that truly permits and directs human self-realization.

It is precisely this that allows us to make an important move. Full-fledged philosophy positively transforms the negation of the negative, but this same transformation leads it to perceive the "something else" that is the true whole of the positive. Philosophy therefore grasps the (positive) difference between its content and the totality of the positive, and thus also between the universal positive (including the pure universal) and the rest of the positive, or rather the positive as such.[98] In philosophical speech the part is positively contained in the whole: philosophy is the pure determination of the whole. From this point of view we could define philosophical discourse as com-positive speech, in the sense that it *puts* different determinations *together positively*. Philosophical speech is therefore integral in the fullest sense of the term, i.e. in the sense that it includes the speaker's strictly personal side, as well as all the aspects that deal with the whole of humanity or the beings with which the speaker has a relation. Philosophical speech is *personal, integral and universally com-positive*.

⑥ Philosophy in the First Person

Autobiography as a philosophical practice. When philosophical discourse becomes personal, it must be performed *in the first person*, but then for this reason we might say that it must be *autobiographical*. At the same time, however, the word "personal" must retain the positive character that we tried to assure through impersonality, i.e. it must be free from conflict with other people's experiences. And here too we begin to see how philosophical discourse fully reunites its two original progenitors, *epistéme* and wisdom: in so far as knowledge

---

[98] In this sense we can perhaps discern in what sense full-fledged philosophy (positively) differs from the Hegelian dialectic: the latter identifies the positive as what differs from all that which is the result of the negation of the negative; the former takes the positive as the result of the negative method of the negation of the negative, including the positive transformation of the negation of the negative.

guides determinate, concrete, personal existence, the full-fledged philosophical knowledge puts this personal dimension at the heart of epistemic truth.

Philosophy appears to be knowledge of integral self, fully fleshed-out and enriched by all of its passions, feelings and experiences; it is an "I" that is philosophical speech's limit, rather than object. The ancient words from the dawn of philosophical wisdom, which conceived of philosophy essentially as self-knowledge, are again applicable. Taking this into consideration, we might follow Pierre Hadot, among others, in saying that our task is to rehabilitate the great experience of traditional philosophical wisdom that characterized ancient Greece – in Stoicism, Epicureanism, Skepticism, etc. – through its inheritance of Socratic teaching.

But at the same time, this outcome is also the natural destination of a line of thinking that confirms and concretizes Western philosophy. It is well known that the figure of the subject has taken on increasing importance in philosophical discourse from Augustine to Descartes, to Kant, through the German idealism of Fichte and Schelling all the way to Hegel. The notion of self-consciousness is decisive and central to the development of modern philosophical thought. Nowadays, the existential, affective "I" has become the center of philosophical discourse, especially through existentialism (Kierkegaard in the 19th century, then Heidegger, Sartre, Camus, etc. in the 20th).

Contemporary, post-existentialist culture is full of examples, particularly literary ones, that show how theoretical reflection and narrative utterance must concern themselves with the existential experience in all of its concrete effectuality and the full reality of its material, sexual, etc. aspects. Female thought in particular has taken on an important role in this regard. I will limit myself to pointing out one of its particularly significant aspects. One of philosophy's principle risks is that it takes as universal something that in reality is a particular determination, in opposition to the other determinations of reality, violently imposing itself on them. Now, female thought most clearly, immediately and understandably denounces this "originary falseness," which claims universality by prejudicially excluding the essential difference of sexuality, and thus of half of the world's population as well.

The philosophical self is the "true," i.e. *real* and still *universal*, "I." But within full-fledged philosophy, what is "true" is free from every negation and exclusion. For this reason, the "real" "I" is *integral*, concrete and enriched by all of its "negative," "material" aspects, by its concrete individuality; it is the "I" *in the first person*; the philosophical "I" *is just me*. The philosopher can speak of truth when he speaks "in the first person [*in der ersten Person*],"[99] as Wittgenstein significantly says about his "Lecture on Ethics." And when the philosopher speaks about "himself" (in Greek: *autós*), his speech can truly be considered "authentic."[100] It is precisely in as much as a philosopher "speaks wholly about himself" that autobiography becomes an essential part of philosophical discourse, which in turn becomes an existential self-interpretation of the self, which obviously contains some type of self-projection.

But in order for the philosophical "I" to be "true" it must be "universal" as well as "real." Except that these two characteristics seem to be irremediably opposed: How can my "I" express itself in its full concreteness without conflicting with other "I"s? As we have seen, the solution lies in the notion of the pure universal. This means that in order for the philosophical "I" to be both real and concrete (and hence autobiographical) without losing its universality, it must be a *pure* self, precisely because it must be free from all conflictual or oppositional negativity.

Nevertheless, if we give a negative interpretation to the word "pure," it is easy gravely to misunderstand the word. On this condition, in fact, purity becomes the *negation* of the *im*-purities of existence, and thus the pure "I" be-

---

[99] This expression can be found in Friedrich Waismann, p. 16, and the notes concern Wittgenstein's "Lecture on Ethics," *ibid*, pp. 3-12.

[100] Clearly, if we stay within the traditional, epistemic, objective conception of truth, it turns out that speaking about the truth in the first person means speaking, albeit wittily, like the first person of the Holy Trinity. Truth is in fact characterized by being definitive and universally binding. The pontifical, arrogant, overbearing and violent nature that philosophical knowledge has assumed derives from this conception of truth. And from this too derives the abandonment of philosophical knowledge for other forms of knowledge. It is only by freeing ourselves from objectivistic necessity that we can speak in the first universal person without falling into egocentric, authoritarian dogmatism.

comes *in*-contaminated, *not* touched by the world's ugliness, or the defects and miseries of existence. But such an "I" would then be "false." The pervasive hostility to this type of purity today is thus fully justified. But in so far as it refuses what is pure, it is trapped within a negative system, even if only in the opposite sense that it substantially accepts, if not quite *favors*, im-*purity*. For example, nowadays we are witnessing an explosion of aggressiveness, which is dangerous for our civilization. We have understood that, in as much as it is the negation of a negative, repressing aggression risks exacerbating the problem. But when we refuse to promote the positivity of peaceful coexistence, we end up confusing aggressiveness with its remedy. From the point of view of "pure self," on the other hand, "accepting" all, even the darkest aspects of our existence does not mean promoting or encouraging them. The autobiography of the pure "I" as we have conceived it then profoundly differs from all *"angiolismo"* of those who claim to present themselves as a reality untouched by the negative; at the same time, it differs too from all renunciations of realizing a purely positive experience.

In such a way, the philosophical self succeeds in finding *a third way* between the negative and the non-negative, and is thus "pure" with respect to the negative in general. We might call this third way "distance:" a distance from both the negative and its denial. It is precisely because of the word's importance in Buddhism that it is particularly apt for illustrating the present situation, especially because it pushes us to understand that what we are distancing ourselves from is *the same "I"* that is taken as the in-deniable limit of authentic experience.[101]

It is worthwhile to point out the paradox of this outcome: in so far as philosophy is autobiography, the "I" seems to take on a central and absolutely

---

[101] When the sage is angry he distances himself in the sense that he has a clear consciousness of the state he is in: he fully accepts it, but by so doing "distances himself" from this way of being. Even in their "negative" formulation, some maxims of Eastern thought are capital here. One is, "You are not this, you are not that, etc." This points to the possibility of distancing oneself from any lived moment, freeing oneself from all negativity. Another is, "You are that:" i.e. you, who are neither your anger, nor your feeling of sadness, nor your desire for something, etc., you are truly *that*, the "pure" that "includes" everything.

privileged role; yet philosophy also radically distances itself from the very "I" in general: *one only fully realizes one's "I" by completely distancing oneself from it*. But this distancing must be quite different from any form of *renouncing* or *denying* the "I," or any form of *in-difference*. Indifference is basically "negativity" with respect to real passions, emotions and feelings. Distance on the other hand is different from any cold and impassible (im-passible) attitude, indeed it makes the passion for the pure existence of things the heart of its own intense, vital affectivity.

If Buddhism is in many ways apt at representing this type of wisdom, Western culture also has figures and moments that meaningfully exemplify it. There is for example the *epoché*, i.e. the state of mind (and here I am thinking particularly of Husserl) by which the subject radically distances itself from all of its mental "constructs" without in any way cancelling or repudiating them. Indeed, they remain wholly present for what they are, but freed from any identification (I mean the identification of the "I" with its conscious lived experiences) that keeps man from real awareness.

In particular, I am thinking of psychoanalysis, one of whose most important, characteristic traits is that it "pitilessly" forces the individual's consciousness to face what its psyche has repressed. We might say that for our purposes psychoanalysis "forces" the individual to become aware of all the "negativity" that composes his history; this same negativity that he has denied, rejected and repressed, and that often ends up causing him enormous disturbances, precisely because it involves the negation of negation. Psychoanalytic therapy functions by differing from the negation of the negative, but also from a pure reappropriation of the negative experience that is the root of the problem. Psychoanalysis is in fact *a third way between the negative and its negation*.

The "first person plural:" autobiography as mythobiography. In so far as the "pure" "I" of philosophy is universal, it is wholly different from any isolated or intimate "I," and consequently philosophical autobiography is something quite different from any exclusive privileging of "privacy" or solipsism. In this regard, contemporary thought has radically questioned the idea that the conscious subject can easily reach its "inside" (see for example Wittgenstein's remarks concerning the "impossibility" of private language). Indeed, psychoanalysis has practically overturned the notion of the subject's self-transparency. In as much as the basis of one's psychic life is in-conscious, by definition it escapes consciousness, and in particular the consciousness to which the unconscious in question belongs. Self-consciousness is not only not easy or immediate, it is in principle almost impossible, or rather it requires at least a third subject (an analyst in the psychoanalytic context) who acts as the medium which allows the "patient" more "objectively" and "truly" to stand before him or herself. Obviously, this "third" element poses a problem, as it runs the risk of simply recycling itself as a new epistemic objectivity, such that the "therapist" ends up having to coincide, at least in some measure, with the patient himself.

Thus the separation between internal and external is no longer applicable, and the same goes for the drastic opposition between my "I" and that of others (and I mean "others" not simply in its anthropological sense). As such, the first person that characterizes philosophical discourse is open and constitutively plural. The others are indispensable for the "I"'s self-interpretation, not only as the third element that is necessary for full self-reflection, but, more radically, they are essential for his autobiography, for they are an integral, constitutive part of his history and of what he is. Thus we can (we must) say that autobiography is truly realized when it places its own single experience within collective, and even universal history, i.e. within what might be called mythobiography:[102] each person's history is the history of everyone else, and universal history is the history of each individual.

It might perhaps be apt to speak of "self-mythobiography." In metaphorical terms, one could see philosophy as a film in which everyone is the protagonist of everyone's story. Or again: a film in which everyone is both character and director at the same time. Obviously this story will be very different from one

---

[102] I take the themes relative to autobiography and mythobiography (as well as others, such as syncretism, solidary self-realization, etc.) from Romano Màdera's disquisitions. I urge the reader to keep in mind, however, that I am here presenting my own reinterpretation of those disquisitions along the philosophical lines that I am tracing.

in which the protagonists are simply heroes, or bosses, or knights, or winners, etc., for those roles are exclusive, and hence exclusionary, and hence negative.

It is significant, in this regard, that contemporary culture accords ever greater importance to very different voices from the historically traditional ones (knights, politicians, warriors), such as those of poets, and of "private" experience, and especially of women. We can say of all this that universal, and therefore solidary, autobiography is characterized and defined by its *omni-centricity*. Omni-centricity is the horizon of philosophical thought; through it each person, and every living being, becomes the center of a system of objective reference. At the same time, a concrete, real individual can only truly be a coherent center if it is a pure self, and hence if it recognizes the same centrality for every other individual, and living being, that it attributes to itself. The individual is truly the center of philosophical knowledge when it accords the same centrality of existence to every other being that it attributes to its own experience.

Universally solidary, or omni-centric, autobiography is obviously universally benevolent. Instead of negating reality's negative aspects, philosophy opts for universal understanding, agreement and compassion, in its etymological sense (*syn-páthos*) of suffering, or feeling, together, and thus also in the sense of *sympathy*. Omni-centrism therefore truly stretches universally: obviously, it concerns human beings first of all, but then, by nature, it spontaneously stretches to all living, sentient beings, and to all beings in general.

Sapiential com-position: philosophical syncretism. These last few considerations highlight the manner in which philosophy resembles forms of spirituality that are not traditionally considered philosophical, such as religious, mystical, sapiential ones: at the apex of its achievement, philosophical knowledge once again coincides with wisdom, with *sophía*.

In so far as this philosophical form of knowledge is omni-centric it is constitutively syncretic. Every existing being is the limit of everything; but in his or her concreteness, every person is essentially incarnated in worldly experiences, convictions, beliefs, religions, institutions, etc.; this means that omni-centrism must hold not only for individuals, but for all cultures and conceptions of the world. Philosophical com-position is also, and especially, cultural com-position.

Obviously a delicate question arises, for different conceptions of the world often appear mutually incompatible, and so a universal perspective seems automatically contradictory. But here too we must imagine our philosophical position as the paradoxical *tertium* that differs not only from the two poles of a binary, but also from a "third" element that is nevertheless in opposition to this binary, or to something at all. Our purely philosophical position differs from every dogma that takes its own conception as the absolute truth, in opposition to all others. But it also differs from any self-proclaimed "neutral" position that opposes dogma, and claims to be universal only because it excludes both poles of a binary (neutral comes from *ne uter*, meaning neither the one nor the other). Our "pure" philosophical position differs from every counter-position, but at the same time, it establishes a positive relationship even with opposing positions.

Thus, given two opposing positions, philosophy certainly seems like something "new," but this "new" can only resolve our difficulties if it is compatible with the positions in question. If it is not, then far from being a "positive" solution, it becomes a new opposing pole that complicates rather than resolves the issue, giving rise to a *regressus in indefinitum*,[103] for now there are three opposing poles, rather than only two.

---

[103] How can we achieve authentic syncretism between two positions that both claim to be the absolute limit of truth (between, for example, a Catholic and a Muslim)? For them, it does not matter much if one recognizes that both of their religions present facets of the truth, or indeed that both may in fact be different expressions of a single truth. The fact is that the Catholic will claim that his position, affirming the divinity and resurrection of Jesus Christ, is a privileged reality with respect to all others, while the Muslim, who nevertheless accords importance to the Gospels and to Christians, will recognize the singleness and exclusivity of Muhammad and the Koran's teaching. A syncretic position that limits itself to recognizing a part of truth in opposing poles ends up becoming a third pole, in conflict with the other two. (And this is what is happening in Western lay society.) Philosophical truth must therefore differ from both of the conflicting positions, but in order to be truly free of all negativity and conflict, it must also differ from any position that opposes both, even if only by excluding some aspect. Here again, we need a *third* position (*tertium datur*), that is third both to both poles of the binary (Christian and Muslim) and to a new binary composed of a third pole in opposition to the first binary.

Truth practices. "True" philosophical theory contains the universal com-position of all determinations, and thus also its own relationship to the rest of reality. But by definition this relationship transcends the theory, taken as a "fixed" object, independent of other determinations. Thus the truth of philosophical theory depends on something that lies beyond "objective" theory, yet it also belongs to it. Thus, while the meaning and truth of philosophical discourse remain to some extent outside this "objective" discourse, they are essential to constituting philosophical *practice*, in which the concrete gesture of philosophical speech takes shape. *The truth of philosophical "theory" depends upon how philosophical discourse is realized.*

From the moment that the content of philosophical discourse is what all the determinations of reality agree to com-pose, then even the relationship that discourse has with the world turns out to be necessary for establishing its value and truth. If the exposition of a philosophical theory conflicts with those to whom it is addressed, it is automatically falsified by its own existence. Conversely, in so far as it creates a free agreement with everyone, it becomes the truthful fulfillment of its own utterance, and from this point of view philosophical practice is emblematic of *self-fulfillment*.[104]

If, therefore, the truth of our philosophical discourse can only be established on the basis of its effective ability to achieve free recognition, it follows that philosophical truth can only be established *concretely*, and therefore, *a posteriori*. In other words, it asks each person, one by one, what he or she thinks about the situation, and takes their replies as "valid," regardless of whether they are negative or positive. On the other hand, once we have gathered that the meaning of a discourse depends upon the concrete use of words and upon the practical context in which it occurs, then linguistic, and more largely, social, practice is the very meaning of the expressions of philosophical discourse. Thus we can say that the *practice* of philosophical speech is a key moment of philosophical

---

[104] This "self-fulfillment" is always partial; all the same, it is only from a negative viewpoint (for which a given truth can be denied by other experiences) that partial truth *cannot coincide* with universal truth.

discourse, for it is essential both for creating its *meaning* and for determining its *truth*.

Philosophy shows itself to be a "composite" activity, but in a further sense than that for which it com-poses, and reconciles, different existences. From the moment that the value of philosophical discourse depends upon how it is concretely "executed," philosophical practice comes to resemble artistic practice: the form and style that present the philosophical word are anything but indifferent and irrelevant for evaluating philosophical discourse itself. For example, philosophical discourse becomes truly *rigorous* when its "gesture" is effectively able to produce a moment of universal, free agreement.

But the way in which a discourse is presented depends essentially upon the nature of the person who proposes it, and thus upon his or her mode of existing wholly and concretely. Thus a philosophy's value is directly proportional to the value of the person who maintains it. And as we are speaking of "purely philosophical" value, the value of the philosophical practice that consists in "stating the truth" will be strictly connected to an individual's practice of self-improvement, i.e. of *self-purification* (self-correction), or of the self-transformation of the real "I" into a purely universal self. The practice of conscious self-improvement, or of the care and cultivation of the purely, universally self-realized self is an essential part of constructing a "true" philosophical theory.

In such a way, philosophy appropriates all of the practices of self-realization and self-clarification that the thousands of years of both Western and Eastern knowledge traditions have made available to humans (such as meditation, prayer, etc.). The syncretism that defines the philosophical experience is valid here too, but in a radical sense, for beyond the traditionally knowledge-based forms of self-realization, such as study, thought, meditation, asceticism, etc., it will have to/will be able to include all the other forms of self-realization as well, especially artistic ones, such as music, recitation, poetry, painting, etc., but more generally too all those that are part of an integrally human experience.

⁊ **Plural Truth: Philosophy as a Communitarian Practice**

Societies of free sharing [con/divisione].[105] If the "truth" of the philosophical word depends upon the positivity of the practical context in which it occurs, then, as a condition of its fulfillment, philosophy demands not only the "goodness" of the gesture that presents it, and therefore of he or she who proposes it, but also the realization of a complete, integral, universal context that allows us to communicate and interpret according to the free agreement that defines philosophy.

The existence of philosophical truth presupposes the establishment of a *philosophical community* whose constituent members relate to one another according to the philosophy's principles. From the moment that a discourse's meaning and truth depend upon the concrete, practical context in which it occurs, and if we truly wish philosophical words to have a universally positive meaning, then they must "come true" *within a real community that is consistent with such a meaning and incarnates its truth.* Indeed, the history of philosophy is full of such examples: the Pythagorean school, or Epicurus' "garden." Or again, there is the political dimension from the pre-Socratics to Socrates and Plato, to Hegel, Marx and beyond, that has forever inspired philosophy and that in some way constitutes its essential, defining traits.

Thus full-fledged philosophical practice fully integrates personal existence into the life of the community. I think it is becoming clear that one of the problems of our political and social life is the division that exists between the existential and personal on the one hand, and the structural and institutional on the other. This division is responsible for the fact that all attempts at improvement turn into their opposite. For a "well-meaning" ["*buonista*"] transformation of the individual that does not consider the real functioning of the objective

---

[105] The Italian word for "sharing" is *condivisione*, which Luigi Vero Tarca writes *con/divisione*, and which he glosses thus: "The spelling *con/division*e is meant to reflect the two senses of *condivisione*: enjoying the same good together, and '*con*-sensual *division*' with regard to situations where this is not possible." [*Translator's note*]

mechanism "shreds" the individual's best intentions in the "meat-grinder" of a system that functions only by rejecting personal needs and "ethical" values.

At the same time, any attempt to reform and strengthen the institutional, objective sphere that does not consider the concreteness of our existence and values exacerbates the submission of single existences to an impersonal, irresponsible, and hence cruel mechanism. Only a social experience in which an individual who is open to self-correction and a community that positively, rather than punitively, offers this correction can produce a real improvement for people and for human life.

In accordance with their original principles, philosophical communities are integral, thus they are constitutionally based on *freedom* and *universality*, on a "law" of the following type: *only that which each member freely recognizes is valid for all members of a philosophical community, and conversely what is valid for one is only that which is valid for all.*[106] These communities are thus guided by a principle of "solidary self-realization:" *the full promotion (self-realization) of everyone is a condition of possibility for each person's self-realization, and conversely, each person's full realization is the condition of possibility for everyone's full realization.*[107]

In accordance with this principle, the constructive criterion of social life for such a community is the "principle of the free sharing of the world:" together we do everything that we agree upon, and together we make use of everything that we agree upon, yet we agree to differ on those aspects whose collective management will lead to disagreement.

I would like to clarify one thing at this point. Very often an intuitive but inconsistent understanding of this principle has led to abuse and violence. For example, someone thinks that he or she has the right to "officiate" over a force-

---

[106] The word "valid" here must be understood as "having *philosophical* value."

[107] In such a way, this principle must be carefully distinguished from the principle that requires the individual to be prepared to sacrifice him or herself for the community. In so far as sacrifice implies a "negation" of the person who offers it, the resulting "universal" good is still a "negative" good. Here however one's own full realization is obviously placed on the same level as that of everyone else.

ful division of *everyone's* property that is objectively and impersonally egalitarian. This automatic, mechanical procedure leads to imposition, authoritarianism, coercion and violence. But this can only occur in a "negative" interpretation of our principle that legitimizes an objective, impersonal and hence illiberal realization.

Now, if it is true on the one hand that from a personal, integral, universal perspective such as the philosophical one, *everything* in principle can be "shared," it is equally true that this "sharing" is rigorously based on freedom. In other words this holds only for those who freely adhere to such a perspective, and even for these people it holds only in so far as each person is freely open to considering something as belonging to the community. So, on the one hand, in principle *everything* falls within the domain of the "care" for the whole philosophical community (and hence this is different from the indifferent or irresponsible one), but on the other, *each person is bound only by that which he or she freely accepts.* Thus such a community can be whole even if from a material point of view very few things are held in common, and thus even if its members continue "normally" to be a part of traditional society.

Thus, truly *doing* philosophy means practicing community life based on these pure principles; in short it means constructing relations and communities of this sort. Precisely because these communities are possible only through free association, they are "elitist" (for it may very well be the case that only very few people are willing to follow the philosophical perspective, given that it is still a determinate, *particular* perspective, even though it aims at universality) and multiple, for they can by definition be built in many different forms. But in so far as this experience is philosophical, it must always be universal and positive, it must be directed at all individuals and the whole society; at the same time, it must maintain a purely positive relationship with each person and with all of society.

Philosophical communities as "purely universal" societies. In so far as philosophical communities are universal and integral, they are also "political." Consequently they face two fundamental problems: identifying the criteria for building a society that can potentially stretch itself universally while still remaining consistent with its own principles; clarifying its own relationship with the given "official" political society.

Well, the criterion for building and unifying a community that is consistent with free universality is obviously "free unanimity:" *a decision is valid for a whole community when it is freely greeted by all the community's members; conversely, it holds for an individual when it holds for every other member of the community as well.*

We often take for granted that such a criterion can only work for small groups or in very particular situations. It is however simply an "optical illusion" that leads us to believe that choosing between a criterion of unanimity and another criterion (for example, majority) is a question of quantity. Two people can be in total disagreement, while in principle thousands of people can be in perfect, free agreement. What we must understand is that free agreement includes consensual division on what might not be agreed upon if we wanted to remain united. Thus, when the members of a philosophical community disagree on a given question, all that they must do is consensually divide themselves into as many subgroups as are necessary for each one to be governed by the criterion of free unanimity.

What often makes adopting this principle as the universal criterion for society appear absurd is that it is automatically referred to already-existing communities that are based on other criteria (nations, schools, neighborhoods, etc.). Thus we are forced to acknowledge that applying the unanimous method to them leads either to paralysis or to forced conformity. But if we reason in this manner, we forget that we thus take societies as objectively given determinations, i.e. as if the "law" that constitutes them were irrelevant to their nature and to the behavior of their members.[108]

From the philosophical point of view, however, a society remains *defined* by the law that institutes it, thus societies whose criterion of belonging is quite

[108] In this circumstance too our perspective's philosophical nature is clear, precisely because it sees determinations as constituted by the law that determines them, instead of taking them as "objective" facts that are achieved independently of the law.

different from the philosophical one are obviously wholly different from philosophical societies. It is therefore natural that they should behave completely differently from what philosophy prescribes. Societies are philosophical when their participants freely and consciously accept free, universal agreement. Thus it only makes sense to wonder whether the criterion of free unanimity can work with respect to this type of society.

On this score, it is worthwhile to observe that, contrary to what we usually assume, the criterion of free unanimity can be applied even when reasons of number, competence or other impose the *delegation* of decision-making. An individual can be authorized to decide in the name of all; it suffices that this delegation of authority be freely recognized by each person for whom he or she decides, and that each person be clear about the limits and weight of the decisions that said individual takes. Thus, in principle, this criterion holds as a rule for building a truly, concretely universal society.

There is a second problem, however, concerning the relationship between this type of society and all others, in particular, those founded on power. Consistently applying our philosophical principle to these societies implies arriving at a consensual "separation" with them, which permits as large a social space as possible that is governed by free agreement. In this way, philosophical societies clearly differ from those based on power, where the conquest of given domains (of power) authorizes the imposition of decisions on all, against the will of some, even by force if necessary. The "philosophical community," however, is based on the principle that only that which each member of the community freely accepts holds for all members.

The political society of power is based on *conflict* and *command* (imposition); the philosophical society is based on *free universal agreement*. Thus these two "institutions" build forms of cohabitation based on their respective principles, and thus their respective *worlds* are deeply different. Moreover, both societies to some degree claim universal value; for this reason they seem to be incompatible. However, this can only happen if the philosophical society conflicts with the society of power, but in this case it would for this very reason contradict its defining principle of universally positive difference.[109]

For this reason, the social experience of philosophy is also *defined* by its ability to have, even with societies of power, relations different from the negative ones, hence different from the relations which cause conflictual or mutually exclusive connections between the two kinds of society. The difference between the political societies of philosophy and of power thus also presupposes their essential co-penetration. From this perspective, "philosophical" society is less an objective, impermeable entity than society's self-purifying trajectory towards freedom from impositivity, conflict and negativity. "Philosophical" society is the glue, the visible and "objectively" individual determination of this trajectory. In this sense, it is rightly the transfisgured descendent of epistemic, philosophical logic, for it preserves all aspects of traditional philosophy (the theological, existential, political, historical, etc.), but transformed through the pure universal.

I would like to bring up one further point. I have been speaking of "philosophical" communities and societies: this is correct in the sense that they consistently derive from the heart of philosophical thought. Nevertheless, if we mean by this that there is something (philosophy) that, or someone (the philosopher) who has a prejudicial (objective), privileged right over human "destinies," then we fall into oppositional logic, where a universal determination is assumed before its effective ability to deal positively with the rest of the world, thus ending up as contradiction and conflict. Clearly it is to some degree correct to say that philosophy permits humanity's universal self-realization, but we must immediately clarify that this means that only that which *in fact concretely* shows itself to be capable here and now of *truly* promoting the solidary self-realization of all of humanity can legitimately be called philosophy.

---

[109] Thus in this case too, philosophical society remains such only as long as it shows that it is able to distinguish itself even from itself as a conflictual pole, thereby achieving a "third" experience with respect to any conflict. (For a definition of "third," I kindly direct the reader to consult note 103.) This formulation obviously holds for any conflict that might arise *within* a philosophical community.

Truth and efficiency. Philosophy understood as the salvific word that fulfills the *epistéme* as *sophia* is the word that speaks free universality, i.e. *it utters both the true and the good word.* But at the same time, it manages this because it is truly able to greet that word in accordance with its content, which is the world based on free universality, i.e. universally solidary self-realization, free sharing of reality. *Fulfilling the philosophical word means achieving a freely, universally shared world.* The philosophical word is the gesture by which the word that announces the advent of the world of free sharing already appears as an example and concrete individualization of this world. The word that says how things "really" stand, *truly*, efficiently "transforms" the world, so that it conforms to the "positive" meaning of its utterance. But at the same time, this word is truly philosophical for it positively transforms the world, allowing it to purify itself of all negatives.

Precisely for this reason philosophy, namely the word true and good at the same time, has the potential to realize the discourse it utters, thus making it *efficient.* Philosophy distinguishes between efficiency and "power" (precisely because power is in principle hardly efficient and is in fact counterproductive for achieving "ethical," wisdom-like [*sapienziale*] values) and therefore appears as the only truly efficient way of realizing justice and peace. The philosophical word is absolutely efficient for it *effectively determines* the reality about which it speaks. And unlike technical efficiency, which is powerful for "objects" but tends to be damaging existentially, philosophical efficiency concerns "ethical, existential" questions. Nevertheless, we must always keep well in mind that the philosophical word's "efficiency" is philosophical only when it shows that it is truly, actually capable of realizing its primary end, which is the full self-realization of all living beings through free, universal agreement. Philosophical "theory" is efficient as long as it *in fact* represents the free, universal agreement and satisfaction of the beings who are the content of its utterance. This means that the manner (the style) in which philosophical "theory" is produced is essential to the ends of evaluating its truth.

Therefore philosophy is an efficient knowledge for it exemplifies the reality whose existence it affirms. Thus, means and ends coincide in philosophy, whereas they do not in objectivistic perspectives based on a dichotomy between means and ends. For these latter formulations, the means is valuable only as a function of the end it must realize. The means may have little or no value, but in so far as it leads to the end, it gains value in accordance with the end's value. Machiavelli's classic saying that the ends justify the means is emblematic of this attitude.

But adhering to his maxim permits and favors the disastrous reversal that we have already seen. In so far as the end *is not* the means, and the means *is not* the end, a bad means that leads to a good end may be more damaging than rewarding. We can only avoid this risk by employing a means that *is* in some way *already* its end, as Gandhi has taught us.

Politics based on impersonal efficiency is destined to become pure military power. This latter is in fact extremely efficient if one wishes to create something for all individuals, independently of each person's free recognition. But only a politics of free, universal agreement can be both efficient and peaceful. It is very far from rejecting the efficiency of Western technical instrumentation (including techniques for managing power), yet it strives to favor the context of general meaning within which alone this technological, institutional progress can truly be a step forward for humanity, rather than a never-before-seen barbarization in the history of animal life on earth.

8 Philosophical Practices as the Valorization and Care for "Beautiful People"

Philosophy as a paradoxically real experience. Philosophical practice can thus be described as *the promotion, valorization and care for "beautiful people."* The word "care" must here be understood in the fullest extent of its meaning: as "therapy" (self-purification), but also in the sense of helping someone to grow, cherishing all of his or her facets, hence worrying about, being responsible for, him or her, and so on. "Beautiful" people are "accomplished" and "fully realized." This means firstly that they have accepted all of their own ugliness, about which they attempt to be as conscious as possible; secondly that they live the full self-realization of other people and of all other beings as an essential moment of their own self-realization. People are truly "beautiful" when everyone else recognizes him or herself in that "beauty," rather than when that beauty overshadows others by making them seem ugly. Someone is really "beautiful" when his or her beauty allows everyone else to appear in his or her own specific beauty.

In this experience and practice, care and attention for the self go hand in hand with care and attention for others and for society as a whole: philosophy consists as much in announcing and realizing *wholly satisfied individuals* as in constituting and nurturing *peaceful, harmonious societies*. This is the "meaning" of philosophical practice. And this is the criterion for measuring the "truth" of its action: Can it truly "form" "beautiful people"? Does it really favor the growth of satisfied, fully self-realized people? Is it a communitarian experience in which this "ideal" is truly evident?

The philosophical experience therefore reveals a decidedly paradoxical turn, for it "com-positively" includes all the factors that tend to oppose each other in "negative" perspectives: it is both *a posteriori* and *a priori*; it is a particular, *determinate* practice with however a *universal* value; it develops in *concrete* people and communities, though it is always an ideal reality that is *different* from any of its concrete "incarnations."

Above we showed how philosophy's effective value depends upon the concrete practice in which it develops: discourse, life practice, the philosophical community. This means that we must understand philosophy as *totally experimental knowledge*, as we must *experiment* in order to achieve an example of philosophy that lives up to its definition. These experiments may succeed or fail, thus we can also say that philosophy is *totally a posteriori* knowledge. In "negative" logic this would mean that nothing in philosophy holds a priori.

Now, it is true that philosophical practice is *instantaneous*, in the sense that it is *always-new* in every circumstance, and hence it is invented and created at every moment. Yet this continual, radical innovation also re-offers a perennial knowledge that always remains the same. In this sense we might say that the current heritage of our philosophical tradition *is* precisely truth; thus in this sense it *holds a priori*. Parmenides' and Plato's texts, the Veda, the Gospels, Buddha's doctrine and so on utter the truth, *they are* the truth, which is as old as the mountains (Gandhi).

And yet they are the truth only when they free themselves of the same negative charge that opposes them to other realities. I would like to say that it is only their ability to free themselves from their very a priori validity (i.e. necessity) that makes them *definitively* true. But conversely, I could also say that, exactly according to their teaching, this freedom is precisely the full realization of their absolute truth, or the realization of what reality truly "must" [*deve*] be. Those "sacred" texts fulfill their identity when they are reinterpreted and renewed in the present. Our heritage of knowledge is effectively handed down when and how those who achieve this "tradition" succeed in "positively" freeing themselves from the whole tradition. One might state this slightly differently, though with no less importance, by saying that we must abandon a sort of fetishism for the written text that easily leads to absolutizing objective, im-personal knowledge in favor of *an oral tradition*, in which the truth of words is handed down alive in the concrete context of an existential, communitarian experience.

The same paradoxical nature that philosophy manifests when it appears as both totally a posteriori and a priori knowledge crops up in the fact that it is a determinate, *particular* practice, which nevertheless claims *universal* value. This seems contradictory, for a partial perspective is claiming an absolute value and total privilege. But this occurs only within a negative point of view, for in the purely universal outlook even the difference between universal philosophical practice and other practices is seen as "pure" difference free of all negativity. Yet this requires that philosophizing be totally permeable to all other practices, and that it co-belong with each of them. Thus, philosophy is consistent with its positively universal inspiration in that it is a *determinate, specific* practice, but *one that recognizes every other practice's claim to universality*. In this sense, *every practice* (meditation, singing, prayer, politics, etc.) is or can be a philosophical practice as well, and can thus legitimately be universal. Philosophical practice is *determinate and specific*, and it *consciously* (explicitly and programmatically) determines the awareness that every single practice must be seen as a manifestation of the possibility of truth, that the philosophical nature of every particular practice must be recognized.

Being a philosopher today: the reality of the ideal. The paradoxical relationship between identity and difference (permeability and distinction) that defines philosophical experience obviously also affects the philosopher. He is surely a flesh and blood person rather than an abstract, im-personal truth, and yet he is truly a philosopher only when he differentiates himself from his objectivistic individuality, i.e. when his philosophical nature is assumed to be guaranteed independently of his effective ability to express the pure universal. The "true" philosopher is made of flesh and blood too, but only if he is a "beautiful person" who can truly give birth to universal self-realization. Everyone is a "philosopher" if he or she consciously gives birth to experiences in which each person truly, concretely manages to live philosophically. An experience that reflects the reality of the ideal of the pure, philosophical universal is authentically philosophical.

This permits us to begin a response to the question that is implicit in the question from which we began: Can there still be philosophers today? And if the answer is yes, who and where are they? If the answer is that the philosopher is a singular, paradoxical *tertium* with respect to every exclusionary opposition (flesh and blood person versus utopian ideal; unrelated individual versus objective institution, and so on), if, that is, the philosopher achieves the positive alterity-co-belonging of every existing being, then we must say, on the one hand, that he exists in flesh and blood people, and therefore in real, effective communities. On the other hand, we must say that what distinguishes this "concreteness" is the essential, originary distinction between the "physical" person (the bearer, *or bearess* of the philosophical discourse) and his or her truly being a philosopher.[110] Philosophical truth is greater than any person, profession, group, institution, society, etc. All the same, it realizes and manifests itself in real, concrete people and gestures: all those who in fact show that they can realize situations of full, existential self-realization and free, universal agreement which are the principle and end of philosophy.

---

[110] It must be clear by now however that in order to think this difference between real person and the figure of the philosopher in a philosophically consistent manner, we must understand that between them there is a "pure" difference, which recognizes that the two can coincide.

Bibliography

Abhinava, Ghupta (1998), *The Tantraloka of Abhinava Ghupta, with Commentary by Rājānaka Jayratha*, Allahabad: Indian Press

Aite, Paolo (2007), *Landscapes of the Psiche Sandplay in Jungian Analysis*, Milan: IPOC

Alighieri, Dante, *The Divine Comedy of Dante Alighieri: Inferno*, tr. Allen Mandelbaum, Berkeley: University of California Press, 1980

Beck, Ulrich:
- (1988), *Das Zeitalter des eigenen Lebens: die Globalisierung der Biographien*, Frankfurt: Rowholt
- (1996), *Individualization and "Precarious Freedoms." Perspectives and Controversies of a Subject-oriented Sociology*, in Paul Heelas, Scott Lash and Paul Morris

Bernhard, Ernst (1969), *Mitobiografia*, Milan: Adelphi

Bodei, Remo (2002), *Destini personali*, Milan: Feltrinelli

Bowlby, John (1982), *Attachment and Loss*, New York: Basic Books

Buber, Martin (1949), *Tales of the Hasidim: The Later Masters*, tr. Olga Marx, New York: Schocken Books

Carrithers, Michael, Collins, Steven, and Lukes, Steven (1985), *The Category of the Person*, Cambridge: Cambridge University Press

Castellana, Franco, Malinconico, Angelo (2002), *Giochi antichi, parole nuove*, Milan: Vivarium

Coppo, Piero (1996), *Etnopsichiatria*, Milan: Il Saggiatore

Cuminetti, Mario (1995), *Per Mario*, various authors, Milan: Linea d'ombra e Libreria Tadino

Debord, Guy (1990), *Comments on the Society of the Spectacle*, tr. Malcolm Imrie, London: Verso

Della Rocca, R. (1994), *Libro di Jonah*, Naples: Tipografia Gaeta

Demetrio, Duccio:
- (1996), *Raccontarsi. L'autobiografia come cura di sé*, Milan: Cortina
- (2000), *L'educazione interiore*, Milan: RCS-La Nuova Italia

Ehrenberg, Alain (1998), *La fatigue d'être soi*, Paris: Odile Jacob

Eibl-Eibesfeldt, Irenäus (1989), *Human Ethology*, New York: Aldine de Gruyter

Ekstrom, Soren R. (2002), "Counterresponse to Jean Knox," in *Journal of Jungian Theory and Practice*, 4:2

Elias, Norbert (1991), *The Society of Individuals*, ed. Michael Schröter, tr. Edmund Jephcott, Oxford: Blackwell

Enzo, Carlo (2002), *Adamo dove sei?*, Milan: Il Saggiatore

Fabris, Adriano (ed.) (2001), *Il tempo dell'inizio*, monographic number of *Teoria*, XXI, 2001, n. 1 (n.s. XI, n.1): 7-45.

Freud, Sigmund:
- (1912), *Remembering, Repeating and Working-through*, in *The Standard Edition of the Complete Psychological Works of Sigmund Freud*, Vol. XII, ed. and tr. James Strachey, London: The Hogarth Press, 1958
- (1916-1917), *Introductory Lectures on Psycho-analysis*, in *The Standard Edition of the Complete Psychological Works of Sigmund Freud*, Part. III, Vol. XVI, ed. and tr. James Strachey, London: The Hogarth Press, 1958

Gabbard, Glen O. (1990), *Psychodynamic Psychiatry in Clinical Practice*, Washington: American Psychiatric Press

Gehlen, Arnold:
- (1964), *Urmensch und Spätkultur: Philosophische Ergebnisse und Aussagen*, Frankfurt: Athenäum Verlag
- (1988), *Man, His Nature and Place in the World*, tr. Clare McMillan and Karl Pillemer, New York: Columbia University Press

Girard, Renè (1982), *The Scapegoat*, tr. Yvonne Freccero, Baltimore: The Johns Hopkins University Press, reprint edition 1989

Hadot, Pierre:
- (1981), *Exercices spirituels et philosophie antique*, Paris: Études augustiniennes
- (1995), *Philosophy as a Way of Life: Spiritual Exercises from Socrates to Foucault*, ed. Arnold Davidson, tr. Michael Chase, Oxford: Blackwell
- (1998), *The Inner Citadel: The Meditations of Marcus Aurelius*, tr. Michael Chase, Cambridge: Harvard University Press
- (2002), *La Philosophie comme manière de vivre*, Paris: Albin Michel

Heelas, Paul, Lash, Scott, and Morris, Paul (1996), *Detraditionalization*, Oxford: Blackwell

Jedlowski, Paolo (2000), *Storie comuni. La narrazione nella vita quotidiana*, Milan: Bruno Mondadori

Jung, C.G.:
- (1929), "Problems of Modern Psychotherapy," in *Collected Works*, vol. 16, eds. Herbert Read, Michael Fordham, Gerhard Adler, New York: Pantheon, 1983
- (1951), *Aion: Researches into the Phenomenology of the Self*, in *The Collected Works of C.G. Jung*, tr. R.F. C. Hull, New York: Pantheon, vol. 9, part 2

Kornblith, Hilary (2002), *Knowledge and its Place in Nature*, Oxford: Clarendon Press

Lagorio, Silvia, Pavoni, Clementina (2001), *Il cocomero rubato*, Milan: Il Saggiatore

Màdera, Romano:
- (1977), *Identità e feticismo*, Milan: Moizzi
- (1996), "La psicoanalisi come sintomo della crisi del patriarcato," in *Rivista di psicologia analitica*, 53:1
- (1997), *L'alchimia ribelle*, Bari: Palomar
- (1998), *C.G. Jung. Biografia e teoria*, Milan: Bruno Mondadori
- (1998), "Non dovevo nascere belva, mamma, io ero fiore," in *Rivista di psicologia analitica*, 57:5
- (1998), *L'animale visionario*, Milan: Il Saggiatore
- (2001), "Lo spirito della narrazione e il Sé," in *Studi Junghiani*, n. 13
- (2002), "A partire dalla pratica analitica del gioco della sabbia: una riconsiderazione della metapsicologia," in Franco Castellana, Angelo Malinconico

Mann, Thomas (1973), "Prelude. Descent into Hell," in Thomas Mann, *Joseph and his Brothers*, tr. H. T. Lowe-Porter, New York: Knopf

Marcuse, Herbert:
- (1956), *Eros and Civilisation: A Philosophical Inquiry into Freud*, London: Routledge and Keegan Paul
- (1964), *One Dimensional Man: Studies in the Ideology of Advanced Industrial Societies*, Boston: Beacon Press

Merton, Thomas (1961), *Mystics and Zen Masters*, New York: Farrar, Strauss and Giroux

Mitchell, Stephen A. (1988), *Relational Concepts in Psychoanalysis:An Integration*, Cambridge: Harvard University Press

Nathan, Tobie (1993), *Fier de n'avoir ni pays ni ami, quelle sottise c'était. Principes d'ethnopsychanalyse*, Grenoble: La Pensée Sauvage

Nathan, Tobie, Stengers, Isabelle (1995), *Médecins et sorciers*, Paris: Empêcheurs de penser en rond

Neumann, Erich (1949), *Tiefenpsychologie und neue Ethik*, Frankfurt: Fischer Verlag, 2001

Pareyson, Luigi (1988), *Filosofia dell'interpretazione*, Turin: Rosenberg & Sellier

Pasqualotto, Giangiorgio (1997), *Illuminismo e illuminazione. La ragione occidentale e gli insegnamenti del Buddha*, Rome: Donzelli

Pinkus, Lucio, Filiberti, Antonio, (2002), *La qualità della morte*, Milan: FrancoAngeli

Progoff, Ira:
- (1975), *At a Journal Workshop: The Basic Text and Guide for Using the Intensive Journal Method*, New York: Dialogue House Library
- (1992), *At a Journal Workshop: Writing to Access the Power of the Unconscious and Evoke Creative Ability*, Los Angeles: J. P. Tarcher

Revelli, Marco (2001), *Oltre il Novecento*, Turin: Einaudi

Riedel, Christoph (1989), *Subjekt und Individuum*, Darmstadt: WBG

Ritsert, Jürgen (2001), *Soziologie des Individuums*, Darmstadt: WBG

Rizzi, Armido (1995), *Il Sacro e il Senso*, Turin: LDC

Samonà, Leonardo (ed.) (2001), *Linguaggi della temporalità*, Palermo: Edizioni della Fondazione nazionale Vito Fazio-Allmayer

Severino, Emanuele:
- (1981), *La struttura originaria*, Milan: Adelphi
- (1982), *Essenza del nichilismo*, Milan: Adelphi
Tarca, Luigi Vero:
- (1993), *Elenchos. Ragione e paradosso nella filosofia contemporanea*, Genoa: Marietti
- (1993), "Il discorso del quale è impossibile pensarne uno migliore. L'argomento ontologico come caso paradigmatico di questione filosofica," in AA.VV., *Dio e la ragione. Anselmo, l'argomento ontologico e la filosofia*, Genoa: Marietti
- (2001a), *Differenza e negazione. Per una filosofia positiva*, Naples: La Città del Sole
- (2001), "Iniziativa filosofica. L'evento del tutto e la possibilità di un sempre-nuovo inizio," in Adriano Fabris
- (2001), "Variazione e negazione. Per pensare il tempo del nichilismo," in Leonardo Samonà
- (2002), "Identità occidentale e pensiero buddhista," in *Dharma. Trimestrale di buddhismo per la pratica e per il dialogo*, 3:9 (April): 58-72 and 3:10 (July): 48-65
Taylor, Charles (1989), *Sources of the Self: The Making of the Modern Identity*, Cambridge: Harvard University Press
Waismann, Friedrich (1965), "Notes on Talks with Wittgenstein," in *The Philosophical Review* LXXIV, 12-16
Wittgenstein, Ludwig:
- (1922), *Tractatus Logico-Philosophicus*, tr. D. F. Pears and B. F. McGuiness, London: Routledge & Kegan Paul, 1961
- (1965), "A Lecture on Ethics," *Philosophical Review*, LXXIV, 1965, p. 3-12
Wuketits, Franz M. (1995), *Die Entdeckung des Verhaltens*, Darmstadt: Wissenschaftliche Buchgesellschaft

Index

Printed in the United Kingdom
by Lightning Source UK Ltd.
123273UK00002B/22-66/A

DATE LOANED	BORROWER'S NAME	DATE RETURNED

Kristine Mann Library
of the Analytical Psychology Club of New York
C.G. Jung Center, 4th Floor
28 E. 39th St.
212-697-7877
info@junglibrary.org

1. Most books are loaned for three weeks, some for one week, and tapes for one week. Please return promptly, or renew in person, by phone, or by email.

2. Overdue items will be fined 10 cents for each day overdue, including Sundays and holidays.

3. When the library is closed, you may return borrowed items to the receptionist or bookstore personnel on the first floor.

4. Borrower is responsible for the cost of replacement or repair of any lost or damaged item.

Please use bookmarks and do not underline,
fold corners, or otherwise deface our books.